It Should
NEVER
Happen Here

Ernest J. Zarra III has taught in Christian and public schools for over sixteen years and has written Christian school Bible and ethics curriculum. He has also served as an associate pastor and short-term missions leader. His graduate degrees have been earned from Simon Greenleaf School of Law, Grace Graduate School, and California State University (Bakersfield). In addition, he has completed studies at Talbot School of Theology and is presently at the University of Southern California finishing a doctoral program. He and his wife and two children reside in Bakersfield, California.

It Should
NEVER
Happen Here

A Guide for Minimizing the Risk of Child Abuse in Ministry

Ernest J. Zarra III

BakerBooks

A Division of Baker Book House Co
Grand Rapids, Michigan 49516

Published by Baker Books
a division of Baker Book House Company
P.O. Box 6287, Grand Rapids, MI 49516-6287

Printed in the United States of America

Library of Congress Cataloging-in-Publication Data
Zarra, Ernest J., 1955-
    It should never happen here : a guide for minimizing the risk of child abuse in ministry / Ernest J. Zarra.
        p.   cm.
    Includes bibliographical references.
    ISBN 0-8010-9031-8 (pbk.)
    1. Church work with children. 2. Child sexual abuse—Prevention. 3. Church personnel management. 4. Employee screening. I. Title.
BV639.C4Z37   1997
259'.22—dc21   97-19478

Scripture quotations are from the NEW AMERICAN STANDARD BIBLE ®. Copyright © The Lockman Foundation 1960, 1962, 1963, 1968, 1971, 1972, 1973, 1975, 1977, 1995. Used by permission.

For information about academic books, resources for Christian leaders, and all new releases available from Baker Book House, visit our web site:
http://www.bakerbooks.com

This book is dedicated to many special people: First and fore-most to the Lord Jesus Christ, whose love, nurture, and warmth toward children is unsurpassed. Second, to survivors of abuse. Remember, "We are more than conquerors in Jesus Christ." Last, to my family, Suzi, Elya, and Jonathan. Words cannot describe my love for you. A special hug to Marjorie. Indeed, "God causes all things to work together for good to those who love God, to those who are called according to His purpose."

Contents

Preface

I began research for this book when I was assigned the task of drafting preliminary screening policies and procedures for a church on the East Coast. The more I read on the subject, the more I was intrigued. My attention was captured by the number of churches that did not think screening was necessary.

This book was about two years in the making. Along the way I heard some tragic stories from children and adults. These stories had one common thread: They were about abuse experienced at the hands of supposed Christians. Some of the abuse took place at church functions and lasted only moments; other victims described years of ongoing, sometimes horrible, abuse.

It Should Never Happen Here is intended to challenge Christian status quo ministry methods. In a day when there are more divorced, single-parent families and more blended families, this book calls the church to rally toward new ministry approaches while affirming the premise that churches are places of security for families.

Shepherds are protectors of lambs as well as grown sheep. There should be no reason to permit a child sexual abuse perpetrator easy access to children. Screening those who will work with children will help to weed out potential problems.

Stephanie Martin, a writer for *Children's Ministry,* challenges churches to tackle this issue head-on as she asks three provocative questions: "Do you have the courage to get involved in the rescue of a child? Do you and your children's ministries staff know the warning signals of child abuse? And do you know what to do if you suspect a child is being abused or mistreated at home or at church?"[1]

Indeed, these are some of the many questions facing the church today. However, the greater challenge comes in the form of this question: Is your ministry willing to move forward on screening before abuse becomes a reality at your church?

Acknowledgments

Personal inspiration for this book came from a variety of sources. The supportive men and women from a very special eastern Baptist church struggled with me as we planted the seed for this book. Their initial insights and questions were a good testing ground.

My wonderful father and mother, whose actions of child advocacy were displayed from my beginning, provided necessary encouragement and motivation to continue onward.

Other special child advocates deserve to be mentioned for their efforts on behalf of children's safety and rights. Thanks Marjorie and Deborah for all your work. The next generation is certainly worth the special attention and concern you give so generously.

I would also like to express my appreciation to the numerous child advocate professionals without whom these pages would never have been written. One very special advocate shared love and concern for children and supplied countless volumes of relevant material. Thanks, Jenny, for your dedication to the children of America.

The faces of thousands of families and children who have touched my life and left more than trace imprints are surely not forgotten. The many children—whose eyes tell their own stories—provide fresh and daily motivation. Their innocence to the ways of the world brings joy to my heart.

Baker Book House deserves credit for its insight into contemporary issues and dedication to publishing a book on this subject. Thank you Paul Engle and Brian Phipps for your professionalism and for believing in this book.

The backbone of the editorial process is Lois Stück, who respected the integrity of my message and wholeheartedly supported the purpose of this book. We both operated by the axiom: "If it saves one child, then it is worth the effort."

Most important, my wife, Suzi, loved, supported, challenged, critiqued, and listened throughout this labor of love. Over twenty years of marriage to this godly woman, and the added blessing of our two children, define the joys of family.

In closing, I wish to express my gratitude in advance to those ministries, churches, camps, mission agencies, Christian schools, and other ministries that decide children need the protection suggested by this book and then face the task of implementation. I will stand beside you both in this world and in the next. Our joy shall be complete now, and then, as we come to understand specific acknowledgment for our Lord, the perfect child advocate, when he says: "Well done, good and faithful servants. Enter into my joy."

-1-

The Need for Screening

Mistrust and disobey,
'Cause I tried the other way.
I'm not happy in Jesus,
And my pain won't go away.

Hymn reworded
by a man abused as a child

Thirty years ago our country was knee-deep in the sexual revolution of the me generation. Some decried the tough moral standards imposed by the Christian church; others lived in open rebellion against them.

Most in the church would agree that the sexual revolution was a precursor to a desensitized approach to sexuality. The acceptance of casual sexual practice, as portrayed in family sitcoms, movies, news programs, talk shows, and advertisements makes a strong case for a correlation. But sex is now more than casual. Today, hard-core pornography is accepted in mainstream America. Child pornography networks exist around the globe. The Internet brims with sex agencies and their wares, not to mention pedophiles and sexual deviates. Everything from lewd discussions in chat rooms to digitally displayed pornographic sex acts can be found on-line.[2]

Recent estimates by research groups indicate that approximately one million children in the United States are abused or neglected, and one child dies every eleven hours due to injuries suffered. Conclusions based on these findings are that one in three girls and one in seven boys will be sexually molested or abused during their childhood years.[3] In this new world of sexual freedom, is it any wonder that our children are at risk?

There are many who debate whether child sexual abuse is on the rise in America. Some speculate that more stringent laws have increased the reporting of abuse, while the actual number of incidents of abuse has remained unchanged. Others claim some accusers are crying wolf and taking advantage of a system with too many loopholes.

Changes in reporting laws have made it easier to report suspected child abuse—even anonymously in some states—but that does not mean people are crying wolf. In 1993 Secretary of Education William Bennett reported a dramatic increase in verified cases of child abuse for every thousand notifications of suspected abuse received by Child Protective Services: from 101 cases in 1976 to 420 in 1991.[4]

Even if child sexual abuse is not increasing, the number of reported incidents is alarming. In 1991 alone, about one-half million cases of child sexual abuse were reported nationwide. Current conservative estimates place the number of children abused between 500,000 and 1.5 million annually.[5]

What clearly is on the rise is the nation's awareness of child sexual abuse. You may recall the McMartin Preschool Case in California (March 1984), in which 354 counts of criminal sexual conduct were handed down against seven of the preschool's workers. Although this case dragged on for over five years, with all charges eventually dropped against all seven defendants, the McMartin case brought the issue of child sexual abuse to the attention of America. Preschools and child care facilities all over the nation worked hard to tighten up their programs and to be found worthy of public trust.

An increasing number of accusations of sexual molestation are also being directed at public and private school teachers, resulting in the adoption of state educational codes addressing appropriate and inappropriate touching. The National Education Association (NEA) and many local teachers' unions now have insurance coverage protecting them against allegations of abuse. Even athletics have not gone untouched. Professional hockey player Sheldon Kennedy (Boston Bruins) revealed that he was sexually abused over three hundred times by a former coach in the Canadian Junior League. After pleading guilty to the charges, the perpetrator was sentenced to three and a half years in prison.[6]

National exposure sometimes results in legislative action to crack down on perpetrators. Sexual abuse cases that have received national attention include the Polly Klaas case in California and the Megan Kanka case in New Jersey. Twelve-year-old Polly Klaas was abducted during a slumber party in her home on October 1, 1993. Richard Allen Davis was convicted of kidnapping, sexually abusing, and murdering her and is presently on death row. At the time of Polly's abduction, Davis had already been convicted twice for kidnapping and assault and was out on parole. This case helped to fuel the drive for California's "Three Strikes and You're Out" criminal legislation reform, which automatically denies parole to anyone convicted of three felonies.

In 1994 seven-year-old Megan Kanka was kidnapped and killed by a convicted sex offender who lived across the street from her. This case resulted in Megan's Law, federal legislation enacted in 1996 that requires sexual offenders to register with their states. Some states also require convicted sex offenders to register with their local communities. Pennsylvania law requires people convicted of sex offenses against children to register their addresses with the state police, which in turn must disclose that information to the neighbors of the sex offender. In California, where there are over sixty-two thousand registered sex offenders, laws permit the police and sheriff departments to release information on sex offenders to the public. Reports of cases like these surface every day in American media.

Churches at Risk

As the nation's awareness of child sexual abuse increases, we in the church[7] must recognize our vulnerability. Churches are easy targets for sexual predators. Legal experts at the Church Law and Tax Report Office verify this assertion. Their conclusion is, "No topic has generated more response than . . . articles on sexual molestation and the church."[8]

Researchers and law officials say wherever children and adults congregate, there is the risk of child abuse. Furthermore, where there exist few measures of protection or screening, there is an increased risk. Child sexual abusers know how to spot programs that grant easy access to children.[9] Churches that are pressured to staff a program with volunteers or place only one person per ministry room invite predators. One incident of child sexual abuse is devastating enough, but since the average child molester will victimize more than sixty children in his or her lifetime, even one perpetrator within the church can cause devastation in the lives of many children.

Since the beginning of the 1990s there has been a significant increase in reports of sexual abuse of children who participated in church ministries or church-related activities, with hundreds of churches facing litigation for abuse or negligence.[10] Reported accusations range from alleged inappropriate touches to multiple sexual acts over the course of many years. Abuse crosses denominational lines and is no respecter of gender or race. For example, the Roman Catholic church has been besieged by allegations and lawsuits accusing priests and layworkers of various acts of molestation and sexual abuse.[11] Some of these accusations are based on occurrences from long ago. Mainline denominations have not escaped either. A former Texas pastor and leader of one of the nation's largest Methodist churches was accused of sexually assaulting eight young women. The seventy-year-old minister denies all accusations, and the case is pending.[12]

In his book *When Child Abuse Comes to Church,* Bill Anderson gives a personal account of abuse incidents with which his church dealt. He wrote the book "to alert the Christian community to the growing problem of child sexual abuse and to educate pastors, church leaders, and parents about the issues and dynamics involved."[13]

Anderson hopes his story "will prepare others to deal wisely with child sexual abuse—either by dealing systematically and effectively with abuse that has occurred or, better yet, by taking preventive measures to keep it from occurring."[14] Anderson's call for prevention is a clear one. The church must be ready to deal with this important issue.

Stranger Danger

Children are taught at an early age to refuse almost everything from strangers. Whether candy, conversation, or car rides, most children are trained to rebuff those whom they do not know. Yet could it be that in teaching our children to beware of strangers, we are actually providing an open door for another type of stranger? Is the church lulled by the safe, secure, Christian ministry environment? Likewise, are children taught that because someone is a Christian, no stranger danger exists?

In about eighty percent of all child abuse cases, the child sexual abuser is someone known to the victim, while strangers account for around twenty percent of reported cases.[15] Richard Hammar writes: "Churches need to be concerned about strangers. But from my experience, the majority of [child abuse] cases have been [perpetrated by] people associated with the church for a long time. It comes as utter shock." Jennifer King (not her real name), former public health nurse and current family visitation counselor for Indiana Child Protective Services, agrees with Hammar. She adds, "One thing you need to know is that child molesters are rarely violent. They work by seduction mostly. Gradually, they entrap the child with more and more contact. They are expert manipulators."[16]

Apparently this lesson was learned a bit too late by one large evangelical church in Southern California. An upstanding elder of the church preyed upon and molested many children over a period of several years.[17] No one in their wildest imagination would have considered this man a sexual abuse perpetrator. He was friendly and popular, and he gained the trust of many over the years. This type of person typifies the new class of stranger—the one whom we all thought we knew!

Another Child Protective Services worker observed, "The cases where the perpetrator appears normal seem to be the rule rather than the exception."[18] She also cautioned that special care should be taken with people who were molested as children. However, we must be clear that just as the fact that most professional football players played football in high school does *not* mean that most high school football players will become professionals, so it is that although most perpetrators were themselves victims of abuse, this does *not* mean that most victims of abuse will become predators.

While there is no one profile that fits all perpetrators of abuse,[19] there are certain types with whom it is best to exercise caution. These include the overly friendly newcomer and the manipulator.

The Overly Friendly Newcomer

One attorney who specializes in child abuse litigation maintains that although there is no single profile of child sexual abusers, her experiences pinpoint the outgoing, highly motivated man. She warned that churches should exercise caution with the man who desires to be at every church function yet bounces from church to church. The following actual case fits the attorney's call for caution.

A twenty-eight-year-old man showed up at services one Sunday at a small church. He was eager to see where God wanted him to minister in the church, so he asked about all the groups that met during the week. His desire was to fit in and find his ministry niche.

After a few weeks of exploration, this young man chose children's ministry. He quickly befriended the pastoral staff and took each to lunch. He became particularly close to the church's Christian education director. Shortly thereafter, the young man was placed in a junior boys' Sunday school class. Everything seemed fine.

Several months later this young man attended a children's summer camp, along with others from the church. While at the camp, a fellow male children's ministries worker observed this young man's loud, fun-loving approach and noticed that it did not go over well with some of the boys. The young man seemed a bit too physical with them, which made the observer uneasy.

As soon as he returned from camp, the concerned worker set up a meeting with the church's senior pastor to explain his concerns. The senior pastor listened attentively but did not share his anxiety. The pastor then explained how he met the new worker and that he fit right in with the church's theological position. In fact he had committed to becoming a member of the small church the next time membership classes were offered. "He might make a good role model for the boys," added the pastor.

Providentially, after further reflection, the pastor called the worker's previous church. He discovered that the young man had been accused by three families of improperly touching their little boys. Although no charges were filed, it appeared that this man's physical approach did little to win the trust of other workers or adult observers. This information prompted the pastor to meet with the young man about the incidents at his former church. Soon after this meeting, the young man left the church and community.

This church did not screen any of its children's ministries workers. Rather, word of mouth, trust in outgoing personalities, and a need for staffing guided the church's decisions. Fortunately, the church was saved from hurt, embarrassment, and a possible child sexual abuse incident, but the close call could have been avoided with screening.

The Manipulator

Sexual predators may target adults as well as children. Manipulative predators search for situations in which they can exercise control over other people. It is wise to question the motives of men who want to be alone with women under the guise of praying together, getting to know them better, or supporting them during difficult times. Churches that tolerate such activities under the guise of ministry risk serious allegations.

I recall one divorced young man who, on separate occasions, manipulated two women into meeting with him in private locations during church support group meetings. First, he suggested that the woman and he share concerns and prayer. These meetings became increasingly intimate. In each case, the woman agreed to brief periods of dating, during which she was pressured into sexual activity with the man.

Manipulation as described here is abusive, whether of adults or children. When we recognize how easy it is for a skilled manipulator to control another adult, it becomes clear that a child could be defenseless against such an abuser. Predators who demonstrate this behavior toward adults should not be involved in children's ministries, but they also should be restricted from adult ministries. Churches should demand that certainly adult ministries workers but especially children's ministries workers be above reproach.

Screening

The goal of screening children's ministries workers is to discourage sexual predators from gaining access to children through involvement in children's ministries. Potential child sexual abuse perpetrators are not likely to attempt to participate in children's ministries because the risk of being screened and found out poses too great a threat. And screening will help a church determine whether a volunteer is an alcoholic, has abused children, has a problem with anger, is on the rebound from drug abuse, or has a criminal record. Word of mouth and informal interviews are just not enough.

For example, a West-Coast Christian school was searching for a vice principal. One applicant was a married man in his midthirties who lived on the East Coast. The school principal interviewed the man, and when he asked why he wanted to move three thousand miles from his home, the man stated that God was leading him to move across the country.

The principal wanted to fill the position quickly, so he became an advocate for the applicant, highly recommending him to the school's board. During the interview, the applicant had mentioned a legal matter that he had to resolve in his home state, but it did not receive much attention because the principal assured the board it would be dealt with swiftly. The board acted on the principal's recommendation and hired the applicant.

Soon after the applicant was hired, his legal problems led to a trial in his home state, where he was charged with and later convicted of child molestation. The school board discovered that he had molested a student while serving as an administrative employee at a Christian school in North Carolina.

Formal screening could have revealed the ongoing legal problems of this administrator. But because the board accepted the principal's recommendation without any unbiased investigation, it was not fully informed of the applicant's background. Bypassing screening and allowing one person to call the shots was much easier, but it made the school vulnerable. In the long run, the easier process is not the safest.

Of course, not everyone is a potential abuser, and the purpose here is not to cause hysteria. Screening is not meant to be invasive; it is meant to be preventive. The probability of an occurrence of child abuse can be reduced nearly to zero by utilizing an effective screening process.

What Are Churches Waiting For?

While preparing this book, I discussed starting the screening of children's ministries workers with dozens of pastors from numerous denominations. Most of the pastors interviewed stated their churches were too understaffed to consider it. Only a few churches did any sort of screening.

What will it take to convince a church, along with its leadership, that screening of children's ministries workers is a necessary component of church ministry and overall church health? Unfortunately, for most churches the answer is either a threat of a lawsuit or an occurrence of child abuse.[20] Only a handful of churches are willing to see screening as actual ministry.

What is it that keeps churches from screening workers? Let us examine some of the objections and challenges. Remember that each should be weighed against the risks of not screening.

Challenge 1: Denial and doubt. "It can never happen here" is the confident assertion of some churches. "Why should we go around mistrusting everyone? The Lord wouldn't! Besides, we're like a family at this church."

Statements of denial and doubt are common responses to screening, especially in smaller churches. No one wants to question the integrity of someone he or she considers family. Nonetheless, the real issue is not mistrusting fellow believers but rather ensuring safety for children and families by discouraging predators from participating in children's ministries.

Challenge 2: Sentiment against intrusion. Across America today there is a growing distrust of everything: the legal system, public education—even the local church. There is also a tendency to resent any intrusion into our personal lives, which is quickly branded as invasion of privacy. Rather than make waves or be labeled witch-hunters by the community, some churches have steered clear of the idea of screening workers. One minister of a smaller independent church summed up the struggle when he said, "It's just not worth the hassle." When a minister, priest, or pastor weighs the risk of making waves with the church board, denomination, or diocese and the probable outcry by members of the congregation, the overworked pastor often concludes that there is, for the moment, more to risk by screening workers than by leaving things as they are.

But a church that does not screen runs the risk of a much larger hassle—one that may truly invade everyone's privacy. If a church is taken to court for an allegation of child sexual abuse, the court will ask many probing questions. The court will push to find whether a church has implemented safeguards to protect its children. If the church has a screening ministry, these questions can be answered with confidence.

Challenge 3: We've always done it this way! Many churches offer programs and services week after week, year after year according to traditional patterns. Ministries operate within certain comfort zones. One associate pastor told me, "In a world where change occurs at breakneck pace, people need a place they can go to where they can count on stability and certainty." This desire for the status quo is more the rule than the exception in American churches today. Church leaders must guard against the tendency to hold traditional ministry lines at the expense of risking harm to children.

If stability is the goal of a church, then screening is a natural fit. What could cause more stability in ministry than the provision of safety for children and security for families? Realistically, nothing would disrupt the way that churches have always done ministry like an accusation of child abuse! Ministries must examine the risks inherent in their practices against the possible loss of ministry, reputation, and money.

Facing the Risks

Whenever a church's actions or inactions have financial implications, pastors usually listen. The possibility of an accusation of child abuse occurring at church may cause a pastor concern, but that concern is intensified when the pastor realizes that great sums of money could be lost as a result.

I recall, however, a lengthy conversation with a friend who is a minister of a large church in a mainline Christian denomination. I explained to him that just one sexual abuse lawsuit against his church would devastate his ministry. Furthermore, if negligence were also charged against the ministry, the church could be ruined, and chances are millions of dollars would be lost. We both understood that a ministry catastrophe would extend beyond the walls of the church to the community and that the lives of those involved would be affected for years. Yet after all our discussion, that church remains uncommitted to the merits of screening.

The fact is that without adequate screening of its workers, churches will be held negligent by the courts. They will be liable for abuse that occurs in its facilities and at its ministry functions, regardless of objection or denial. Losses of reputation and ministry would likely follow as well as the financial losses.

But the church today is gambling with something much more valuable than money. The church is taking chances with children and families. The lack of screening places churches in risky situations with the odds against them. By its inaction, the church sends a message that the gamble with our children is worth taking.

Our Lord would never have tolerated an adult's sinful actions upon a child. Therefore, it is logical to assume that if he walked the earth today, Jesus would be in favor of screening those who work with them.

Jesus' position on children is clear:

> "But whoever causes one of these little ones who believe in Me to stumble, it is better for him that a heavy millstone be hung

around his neck, and that he be drowned in the depth of the sea. Woe to the world because of its stumbling blocks! For it is inevitable that stumbling blocks come; but woe to that man through whom the stumbling block comes!"

Matthew 18:6–7

The church is Jesus' body, and as such, it is called to protect its little ones. Yet, by not implementing worker screening, many churches act contrary to their convictions. When children are sexually abused—particularly when that abuse occurs in connection with the church—they can be caused to stumble to the extent that they are kept from having a vibrant relationship with God.

The corporate church should do all it can to make certain that nothing gets in the way of the little ones coming to Jesus. The screening of children's ministries workers is one way to accomplish this. Screening should be seen as a way to lead children into a safe and meaningful relationship of trust with Jesus.

Part 1

Screening Children's Ministries Workers

Once we are convinced of the need for screening children's ministries workers, what are the next steps? How can we best introduce screening to the congregation or ministry team to gain trust and support? What exactly is involved in screening? Who will make the decisions? What does the application process entail?

These and many more questions will be answered as we examine how screening works. In part 1, we will look at how to implement screening in your church or ministry, how to select the screening committee, and how to carry out the primary and secondary phases of the screening process.

-2-

Implementing a Screening Ministry

Like a shepherd He will tend His flock,
In His arm He will gather the lambs,
And carry them in His bosom;
He will gently lead the nursing ewes.

Isaiah 40:11

Change is a word that ministries do not like to hear. Even the smallest changes in ministry programs or methods may encounter stiff opposition, often simply because people like the security and stability of the status quo. Screening of children's ministries workers definitely is seen as a big change by most churches. Therefore, leaders must promote the change in advance. Actual implementation of a screening program may have to begin with laying the groundwork for change, using the same tact and sensitivity given to all other delicate issues with which ministry leaders are accustomed to dealing.

Each church or ministry has its own governing system, and the first step is to win the support of the decision-makers. In some cases this responsibility will rest with an individual leader, pastoral staff, board of directors, or elders. Others will require the vote of all members or by a diocese or other governing body. If the decision rests with an individual pastor or ministry leader, that person needs to know that screening will not overwhelm an already overly busy leader. Rather, after making the decision to screen and overseeing the setting up of the ministry, the process can practically run itself. If the decision rests with a larger governing body or a vote of the membership, it might require adapting the suggestions in this chapter to an information campaign. Whatever process is necessary, the result of providing a safer place for children will be worth the effort.

Keys to Success

Once the appropriate body has made the decision to screen children's ministries workers, the successful implementation of this bold new ministry requires a plan of action. And the success of that plan depends on how well ministry leaders incorporate the following key elements.

Do your homework. Accurate supporting information is key to winning over skeptics to the whole idea of screening. Useful sources of information are daily newspapers, local bookstores, child protective services, and testimonies of fellow believers. Appendix 4 lists both secular and Christian organizations as well as Internet sites that can provide information and statistics on child abuse. The *Journal of Interpersonal Violence* relates many relevant anecdotes. Other supporting information can be obtained through reading autobiographies of survivors or books on counseling (check with your local bookstore) and journals such as *Christianity Today.* Counselors in your community may also be an excellent source of information and support.

Consult legal and financial experts. Ministry leaders ought to utilize the ministry's lawyer and insurance agent. These individuals have an important perspective on the legal implications of a sex abuse incident for a ministry. In addition, people listen to experts. Ministry leaders' stance on screening can be strengthened by the advice of experts in these fields.

Preparation and prevention are the best ways to minimize the risk of abuse. A ministry should not wait for a tragedy before it consults with a lawyer. Any ministry can benefit from the advice of an experienced, mature Christian attorney. If it is not financially possible to have a lawyer on retainer, the church may be able to consult a member who is an attorney. Or Christian Legal Services and the Christian Law and Tax Report Office can recommend many excellent Christian lawyers—some of whom may even offer free advice.[21]

Sometimes dissension may arise over bringing in a legal expert. Some skeptics may feel screening is not worth the cost of an attorney. Others may not trust lawyers or may feel that seeking legal advice damages the reputation of a ministry by giving the perception that there is something wrong. Fortunately, such dissent usually dissipates when confronted with the potential financial loss and damage to the ministry's reputation if an incident of abuse were to occur. In the final analysis, few people will want to take a stand against safeguarding children.

Contact other ministries. Ministry leaders would do well to consult with other ministers to learn their position on screening. Colleagues can share concerns about screening and ideas that have proved successful as well as ways they have dealt with problems. Such conversations can lead to the refinement of screening efforts. As a side benefit, leaders who share screening ideas with one another may begin to sense unity in purpose rather than competition in programs. Churches, in particular, may begin to turn a sympathetic ear toward each other's ministries.

Communicate fact with tact. Ministry leaders must communicate information with tact, gentleness, and a loving spirit. "A gentle answer turns away wrath, but a harsh word stirs up anger. The tongue of the wise makes knowledge acceptable" (Prov. 15:1–2). Communicating to a group of people the ministry's concerns about the sensitive issue of child abuse will certainly be a challenge. Pastors and other ministry leaders should remember to speak fact with tact.

Obtain pastoral support. Any effort to implement a screening program must have the support of the ministry leadership. This will be most easily accomplished when the pastor has a people-oriented rather than task-oriented philosophy of ministry. Such a pastor will more quickly accept screening as an important ministry in the Lord's work rather than simply another program or exercise. Even a pastor reluctant to support screening may yet be convinced by the successes of other ministries that use screening as well as by accounts of the harm done to a church by an incident of abuse. (See chapter 1 for examples and references.)

It is then the pastor's responsibility to lay the groundwork for convincing the congregation of the need for screening. Again, seeing screening as ministry can be crucial to success. When there is major opposition to implementing screening, it usually is because the leaders did not adequately communicate this philosophy.

A Plan of Action

In addition to the above keys to success, good timing is essential in gaining a positive response to screening. The people must be brought into the process with adequate information and the time to understand and accept it. The following is a suggested three-month plan for introducing screening to your church or ministry. It can be adapted to meet the personality and needs of your congregation or group.

Month 1	Weeks 1–2	Announce the move to screen children's ministries workers and the reasons for doing so. Begin selecting screening committee members.
	Weeks 3–4	Hold churchwide question and answer meetings.
Month 2	Week 1	Allow the congregation to review the screening forms.
	Week 2	Hold another churchwide question and answer meeting.

Week 3	Introduce the screening committee. Have workers give testimonies in support of screening.
Week 4	Have a special recognition Sunday to honor children and children's ministries workers.
Month 3	Begin screening workers who are already involved in children's ministries and any new applicants. Give priority to those working with the youngest children and work up.

The First Month

Weeks 1–2: Announce the Move to Screening

Begin implementing screening by distributing a written pastoral announcement of the move to screen workers. The pastor (or ministry leader) should state briefly and clearly the need for screening and why it is a churchwide ministry concern. At some time during these two weeks, the leadership should give the congregation a tentative calendar for the steps that will be taken during the three-month period.

The senior pastor should also write one or more articles in support of the screening process and publish them in the church's weekly, monthly, or quarterly newsletter, or perhaps in some other form, such as a small booklet. This kind of communication can be key to convincing many that screening volunteer workers is essential.

The pastor should carefully select the information included in the written announcement and articles of support. A balanced presentation is important. The pastor should avoid giving the impression that there is panic among the staff about the issue of child sexual abuse. The pastor should also avoid sending messages like "our church has a problem" or "we are watching the members of the congregation very closely." These writings must emphasize safety and provide data and biblical support to justify the screening process. Consider the following suggestions.

Cite recent, accurate national and local statistics about child sexual abuse and child abuse in general.

Present biblical principles to supply the impetus for churches to ensure their ministries provide a healthy, secure environment for children.

Challenge the idea that child sexual abuse "could never happen at our church." Cite incidents from other ministries that thought the same thing.

Announce a special recognition Sunday to honor children and children's ministries workers.

Bring the point to a personal level by expressing the pastor's heartfelt concern for the flock and by relating stories of lives harmed by abuse.

Address the church's liability in a child sexual abuse incident from the legal and financial points of view. Consider printing a booklet specifically discussing liability, negligence, and the legal benefits of screening.

Impress upon the congregation the importance of confidentiality during the process of screening to respect the privacy of applicants.

Explain what measures will be taken to ensure that application information will remain strictly confidential.

Explain why screening is a ministry.

Promote preventive ministry. Use the theme "It should never happen here."

Once the screening process has been introduced to the congregation, it is time to begin selecting the screening committee. (See chapter 3 for a detailed discussion of the selection process.)

Ministries will vary on how quickly they act, depending on size and level of support for screening. The time line can be adjusted to fit each ministry's situation.

Weeks 3–4: Hold Question and Answer Meetings

The second half of the first month is an excellent time for churchwide question and answer meetings. The number of meetings will depend on how long it takes to address the concerns of the congregation. The church leadership should be present at all of these meetings and could invite the church's attorney and a representative from the church's insurance company to attend one or more of the sessions.

The Second Month

Week 1: Congregation Reviews Screening Form

During week 1, have the adult members of the congregation preview the Children's Ministries Worker Application and the Children's Ministries Rescreening Form. (See appendix 1 for sample forms.) In order for the process of screening to be successful, the people of the church must take ownership of it. Soliciting the congregation's feedback on these forms helps accomplish this goal. The general examination of the screening forms provides two other benefits: It enables the congregation to move toward unity, and feedback from members can benefit the application process by providing the impetus for necessary revisions. Smaller churches that involve their congregations in this way may experience a higher degree of acceptance of the screening process.

Larger churches, however, may find that involving the entire congregation is simply not practical. For example, if each member of a one-thousand-member church submits comments on the forms, the review process will barely creep forward. Certainly each member should have access to the forms, but larger churches might consider randomly selecting members of the congregation to serve as reviewers and suggest improvements.

Week 2: Hold Another Question and Answer Meeting

Another churchwide question and answer meeting at this time allows the church leadership to address feedback on the screening forms given by the congregation or the randomly selected reviewers. After this meeting, leaders will make any necessary revisions.

Week 3: Introduce the Screening Committee

Although it is suggested that the screening committee be selected during the first month and introduced during week 3 of the second month, remember that this schedule can be modified to meet the needs of each church or ministry. Rushing the selection of committee members in order to meet a deadline could jeopardize the reliability of the screening process. It is important that selection begin only after the leadership has given its full support and the congregation has been introduced to the concept of screening. This will avoid negative feelings that could ensue if word got out that committee members were selected before the congregation had accepted the idea.

Each church must weigh for itself the best method for presenting the screening committee to the congregation. Some churches might call each of the screening committee members to the platform for introductions and an official commissioning ceremony. Others might ask that committee members come to the front of the church at the end of a service so that people can meet them informally. Still others might opt to make an announcement in a Sunday bulletin or place a handout at the entrance of the building.

Whatever method is chosen, it is important that the committee is introduced to the congregation before screening begins. Doing so gives the church body a chance to show support for the process. More important, it provides the opportunity for an informal screening of the committee. After the announcement of the committee members, a two-week waiting period is recommended prior to commencement of screening committee ministry. It should be made clear to the congregation that during this time, they can bring concerns about a committee member to the senior ministry staff. Assurances should be made that all information will remain confidential and that this is not an attempt to embarrass anyone but simply to stress the importance of caution in selecting a reliable screening committee. If a person has been placed on the committee who for some reason is not fit to serve, it stands to reason that someone in the congregation will help correct the oversight.

In addition to introducing the members of the screening committee, during this week's Sunday morning service the church could present testimonies to support the screening process. The pastor could choose the type of testimonies most appropriate to his or her church: adults recovering from child sexual abuse, repentant perpetrators, children's ministry workers, parents, or even children. Those chosen should address the need for safety in the ministry.

Week 4: Have a Special Recognition Sunday

Promote week 4 as "Focus on Children's Ministries Week." On Sunday morning, the pastor could preach on "the need for protecting our children." Set up creative decorations along with information booths, carts, or tables. Make buttons to show support of children and those who minister to them. Have the Christian education pastor call workers forward or have them stand to be applauded for their faithful efforts with children. The show of support for children's ministries workers will ultimately strengthen support for the screening process.

Pastors could use the following outline for preparing the sermon. This outline could be given to all churchgoers on this day. Some churches may also want to provide a response sheet for feedback on screening, which members could leave at the back of the sanctuary at the end of the service.

Suggested Sermon Outline
Title: "Protecting Our Children"
Primary Text: Matthew 18:1–14

I. Introduction: The Need for Protecting Our Children Today
   A. Recent News Reports of Abuse
   B. Statistics from Agencies
   C. Church Lawsuits

II. What If the Church Does Not Screen?
   A. Ministry Implications
   B. Legal Implications
   C. Biblical Principles Violated
   D. Responsibility of the Church to Protect Children

III. Steps to Providing the Safest Church for Children and Families
   A. Screening of All Children's Ministries Workers
   B. Congregational Support Needed
   C. Overview of the Process of Screening
   D. Introduce the Timetable for Beginning the Screening Process

IV. Conclusion
   A. Testimonies of Children's Ministries Workers and Children
   B. Prayer for the Screening Committee and Unity of the Church
   C. Why Child Sexual Abuse Should Never Happen Here

The Third Month

Begin Screening

Begin the screening process by distributing the Children's Ministries Worker Application to all children's ministries workers and potential new workers. The following table offers five approaches that could help expedite this process.

Distribution Method	Strengths	Weaknesses
	Method 1:	
A pastor distributes applications at a meeting of all children's ministries workers and explains the screening process.	Face-to-face distribution and explanation of the application. All workers review material in a larger group setting.	Workers may face some apprehension in a larger group led by a pastor.
	Method 2:	
A pastor distributes applications to smaller, departmental groups. This method is highly recommended.	More personalized distribution of applications; questions and answers seem less threatening.	Takes more time to meet with numerous smaller groups.
	Method 3:	
Designated church board member or experienced liaison distributes applications in place of the pastor.	Connects distribution process to other church leaders; frees up pastors to use time for other areas of ministry.	Some church leaders may not have the same passion for screening as pastors overseeing children's programs. This person must have the respect of the congregation and be able to answer questions about the process.
	Method 4:	
Distribute applications through the mail to all children's ministries workers and new applicants with a cover letter to explain the process.	Simple and quick method with good blanket coverage.	Impersonal approach. Risk of recipients not reading material completely; telephone calls may flood the church office; mailing can lead to extra expense. May also require an accompanying pamphlet that answers basic questions, such as privacy issues, reasons certain questions are asked, and why screening is necessary.

Distribution Method	Strengths	Weaknesses
Method 5:		
Describe the screening process in the church membership class and make applications available.	Sets precedent for all newcomers and establishes screening as an important facet of church ministry.	Leaves established membership out of the process. Would have to be combined with one of the other methods to reach all who attend the church.

Completed application forms must be handled with the utmost of care or the integrity of the entire screening process and the privacy of the applicants will be jeopardized. Each applicant should be given an envelope along with the application. To ensure privacy, applicants should put the completed form in the envelope, seal it, and place it into a secure collection container designated for that purpose. This container should be accessible to the average person in the church but away from general church traffic, preferably not in the main church office. Placing it inside the office of the senior pastor, Christian education director, or Sunday school superintendent will add to the feeling of confidentiality. If possible, use an offering box with a slot large enough for the envelopes but locked for security.

A pastor or an elder should be designated to oversee the collection of the forms. He or she will give the sealed envelopes directly to a designated member of the screening committee. The success of the screening process will be compromised if applicants believe their applications are being mishandled; therefore, the forms should never leave the church building. They should be stored in a locked file cabinet except when the screening committee is reviewing them.

The efficiency of the application process is a main concern of the screening committee. The timeliness of the screening process depends on the prompt return of the completed applications. Each applicant should be given a fair amount of time to complete and return the form—under normal circumstances a period of two weeks is generally acceptable. If a person does not return the completed form by the deadline, someone should telephone the applicant. The applicant could be given an extension but be notified that if the form is not submitted within the allotted time, his or her name will be removed from consideration.

Some churches may want to permit their members to fill out worker applications by computer. A church could make the form available on a computer, and the applicant could either (1) access the form using his or her own computer or (2) come to the church and fill out the form on the church's computer. Some churches might even encourage applicants to use electronic mail or facsimile machines to submit their applications, but these methods will also increase concerns for privacy. Churches using such technology or developing new and creative approaches for distributing and collecting applications must be careful to ensure the privacy of applicants. Ministries should steer clear of methods that are aimed only at cutting corners or saving time. Shortcuts may save time or money, but they may also weaken a ministry's position if it ever faces litigation.

Pray for the Process

The church should be committed to praying for the screening process. Specifically, pray regularly for the screening committee, children's ministries workers and new applicants, and the church's families and their children. If a church has not had to deal with a child sexual abuse incident, it should praise the Lord and offer thanks.

During this third month the church might consider inviting the local community to join in supporting its efforts to protect children. Involvement of the community is not essential to the success of a church's screening program, but a ministry that is concerned for the safety of children and families is seen as a safer, more attractive place. This message can add to the outreach of the church.

Of course, each church must decide how much community involvement is appropriate. The purposes can range from promotion of the ministry, to introduction of safety issues to the community, to evangelism or outreach. Depending on the size and interests of the church and its surrounding community, these purposes can be accomplished in a variety of ways, including door-to-door flier distribution, informal meetings in homes, or larger rallies. A church could also sponsor a seminar with a child-advocate professional. The local media could be invited to attend seminars or rallies. A newspaper article, television coverage, or radio announcement would reach a broader audience with the church's message and enhance the church's reputation.

Once the community senses that a church or ministry is out front on an issue, it might consider that the church's other messages are also worth hearing. The church becomes a light in the community when it shows tangibly that it is genuinely concerned about children and families.

-3-

The Screening Committee

> But we request of you, brethren, that you appreciate those who
> diligently labor among you, and have charge over you in the Lord
> and give you instruction, and that you esteem them very highly in
> love because of their work. Live in peace with one another.
>
> 1 Thessalonians 5:12–13

The success of your ministry's screening program will rest on the shoulders of some very important people—the members of the screening committee. These people will examine applications and check references to determine who will be allowed to minister to children. For this reason, committee members must be chosen with great care. They should be men and women who possess appropriate Christian maturity, compassion, and sensitivity toward the issues of abuse as well as a strong respect for confidentiality.

Those who will serve on a screening committee face an awesome task. An equally imposing task is faced by those leaders who choose the members of the screening committee. The task of assembling, empowering, and supporting a screening committee is an important one. In some churches, the committee members will be chosen by the elders. In others, the responsibility might fall to the deacons or trustees. In most cases, decisions to place people in a screening committee will be made by the ruling board of the church or ministry. In any case, these leaders should strive to be impartial, not allowing church politics, favoritism, or nepotism to influence their decisions. If the congregation trusts the church leaders, this will translate into confidence in and respect for the screening committee. Above all, the process of assembling a screening committee should be committed to earnest prayer.

General Qualifications

Those on whom the responsibility of screening rests must be of good reputation in the church and in their local community. Having a perpetrator or even someone with loose morals on the screening committee would taint the decisions of the committee because such a person could not be trusted to make the best decisions regarding protecting children from abuse. For this reason, it is wise to have the screening committee made up of official members of the church. Though requiring church membership is not a guarantee against a person being a child abuser, the process of becoming a member may in effect serve to screen potential committee members. In churches where membership is not required, even more careful attention should be paid to the general qualifications listed in this chapter.

Be cautious not to overload the committee with any one personality type. Having too many task-oriented people could result in a routine, project-centered approach; on the other hand, a people-oriented screening committee runs the risk of decision-making paralysis for fear of negative comments and unpopularity. And members with excessively pastoral hearts may refuse to reject an application for fear of causing further hurt or pain in someone's life, while the critical, analytical type might be too ready to find fault. What is needed is a complementary balance of members who can work together to identify problems and reach decisions.

Other more specific qualifications of screening committee members parallel the traits of church elders (see 1 Timothy 3). Besides character areas such as a good reputation and Christian maturity, good communication and teamwork skills are also crucial to the success of the screening committee's ministry. As we examine several traits recommended for screening committee members, consider which individuals in your church or ministry exhibit these characteristics.

Confidentiality. In order for the corporate church body or ministry to accept the screening process, it will be crucial that the screening committee hold to the highest standard of confidentiality. Does the candidate possess the ability to keep information confidential? Has he or she proven to be a reliable and trusted confidant in the past, or does the candidate have a reputation of speaking too freely or gossiping? Serious consideration should be given to these questions.

Teamwork. A team is composed of members striving toward the same goal. Two of the goals of the screening committee should be: (1) the safety and security of children and families and (2) the assembly of a quality children's ministries staff. In order to attain these goals, the committee must be unified.

This is not the place for the highly opinionated individual, who might make disagreements divisive. Candidates for the screening committee must be people who can work as a team in spite of different viewpoints. They should understand that disagreements, rather than necessarily being negative in nature, can give new perspective and clarification to issues.

Reputation. All screening committee members must be of good reputation in all areas of their lives. They must be well thought of in their families, among their friends, at their place of employment, as well as at church. There can be no hint of double standards or unscrupulous behavior for someone who will be passing judgment on the character of others. A trustworthy reputation is of paramount importance.

Clear thinking. Members of the screening committee should possess the ability to assess information and reach reasonable conclusions. The "very nice person" who lacks the ability to articulate an opinion or to think fairly and clearly is not a wise choice for the screening committee. On the other hand, those who jump to conclusions can cripple a screening committee just as much as those who are unable to reach conclusions.

Tact. No matter what the circumstances, applicants must always be given respect and consideration. Screening committee members must be able to put aside personal issues and work together as a team to deal tactfully with people, no matter how difficult the situation. They must have the grace to make it clear that rejection of an application is not a rejection of the applicant. In some cases, it may be necessary to recommend to an applicant that he or she should make an appointment with a pastor or counselor. This must also be handled tactfully and lovingly because the tactful way in which each life is touched is an important part of the ministry of the screening committee.

No conflicts of interest. A screening committee member should be free of any major conflict of interest in the church. It is wise to have children's ministries screeners who do not serve in any other church ministry, although this may be impossible in small churches. Ideally, screeners also should not be spouses of those who serve in the ministries that will be impacted by their decisions. It is virtually impossible to be impartial when screening a spouse or even a close friend. On the other hand, it is also important that screeners not have unresolved conflicts with people in the church.

Another major conflict of interest may arise if pastors who oversee children's ministries programs serve as screening committee members. A pastor who feels pressured to staff the Sunday school might coerce the committee to act quickly rather than carefully.

Professional experience. Although not a requirement, certain types of professional experience will benefit the screening process. Has the candidate worked in law enforcement or as a counselor, educator, or pastor? Are any people in the church social workers, human resources personnel, or child advocate professionals? These individuals may have insight into the nature and problems of people.

One caution should be noted at this point. A screening committee made up only of professionals could cause some ministry concerns. First, some professionals might not perceive their screening tasks as ministry, confusing ministry tasks with those of their professions. Second, screening committee members must always remember to find their motivation in Jesus Christ rather than in the priorities of their profession, because their decisions will impact many lives.

Christian maturity. Screening committee members must be believers in Jesus Christ and display Christian maturity. This is important because mature ministry decisions necessitate the knowledge and application of biblical principles. Screening committee members must be those who exhibit maturity through years of discernment and growth, through which wisdom, fairness, and compassion blossom. New believers should not be put in the position of screening others much more mature in their faith. There are many other ministries in the church that are more appropriate for new Christians.

As you consider candidates for the screening ministry, carefully weigh the following questions:

Are the candidates respected in the local community as well as in the church?

Will the candidates be able to operate as a team, even in the face of disagreement?

Will confidentiality be a problem for any of the potential screeners?

Are the candidates tactful and inoffensive in their approach to others?

Is their wisdom and experience helpful and insightful?

Would they know what to look for on an application or in an interview?

Is there any conflict of interest on the part of any potential screeners?

Do they have professional experience that would be helpful
to the screening process?

Are the candidates mature in the Lord to make wise decisions?

Is each potential screener able to overcome the feelings that
accompany the rejection of an application?

Forming a Team

After the move to screening has been announced to the congregation (see chapter 2), the ruling board should compile a
list of no more than ten qualified candidates for the screening
committee. From that list, the board will later choose five to
seven people to serve on the committee. Fewer than five members causes an overload of work, which can result in glossing
over applications. More than seven can pose problems in reach-
ing a consensus.

Once the final list is compiled, church or ministry leaders
should contact the candidates to inform them of their candidacy
and to provide an overview of the screening process. Do not pres-
sure them to decide immediately whether they want to accept
their nomination. Candidates should be given time to consider
the matter through prayer and reflection.

Be sure to inform candidates of the length of time they will
be expected to serve. Two- or three-year terms seem to work
well, although this is best left up to individual churches or ministries. Some may choose to rotate new screeners in every year,
but an annual rotation method does not provide the continuity
or cohesiveness that multiyear terms provide. Other ministries
may want the screening committee terms to be the same as those
of their board members, elders, or deacons. Another option is
to combine screening terms of two and three years in length,
staggering them to avoid a complete turnover of members. Careful planning can ensure that one or more experienced screeners
remain on the committee when the terms of other members

expire. In any case, this decision should be made prior to approaching candidates, so they can make informed decisions.

Once a candidate agrees to serve on the screening committee, he or she must fill out a Children's Ministries Worker Application and be screened by the ruling board of the church and the pastoral staff. This screening provides necessary security and integrity from the very beginning and serves as an example to others within the church.

All screening committee applicants must also be willing to submit to a background check, which may include fingerprinting by a law enforcement agency. This is best accomplished early on in the process, so as to save embarrassment for anyone who might choose to remove his or her name from consideration. It is essential to scrutinize screening committee candidates; however, it is important to remember that background checks are never excuses for nosing around the personal affairs of others. Candidates must be assured that all information from the background checks will remain confidential.

This more formal screening, as well as the informal screening of introducing the members to the congregation (see chapter 2), is necessary to give the committee validity. By submitting to screening themselves, they witness to the importance of the process. It also minimizes the chance that a secret perpetrator could be on the committee, which could invalidate the screening process.

Along with the selection of screening committee members, at least one member of the ruling board of the church should be appointed to serve as liaison to the screening committee. The liaison is not an actual member of the screening committee, but he or she should be available to attend screening committee meetings as needed. Some churches may choose to have the liaison meet regularly with the screening committee as an adviser.

After the screening committee has been selected and introduced to the congregation, the first task of the committee should be to appoint a chairperson. Next the committee needs to:

1. *Lay out a schedule for screening present workers and new volunteers.* As shown in the three-month plan for implementation in chapter 2, it is best if the screening process begins within a few weeks of the selection of the committee. The process of primary phase screening is described in detail in chapter 4.

2. *Assign responsibilities to screening committee members.* Besides a chairperson, the committee will need a secretary to record the minutes and someone who will regularly collect applications. Another person could be appointed to handle telephone calls to remind applicants of deadlines or request clarifications. There should also be a devotions leader, who will keep the committee's focus spiritual.

3. *Determine how often the committee should meet.* The committee should meet at least twice a year, though quarterly meetings are preferable. Meeting quarterly will help the committee keep up-to-date and better informed. At first the committee might need to meet more frequently because the burden of screening is always heaviest at the front end. However, after the initial surge, screening will become more of a maintenance-level load.

Decisions of screeners have a lasting impact on the applicants, and mishandled decisions can produce major conflicts. However, a screening committee that is thorough and fair in its dealings with people will incur little criticism.

The screening process takes time, and committee members will be required to make difficult decisions. Whenever doubts or criticism arise, keep in mind the big picture and ask yourself, "What damage would be done to a child as the result of a sex abuse incident? And what would happen to the church or ministry in light of such an allegation or incident?" The bigger picture is more important than any criticism.

-4-

The Screening Process

Obey your leaders, and submit to them; for they keep watch over your souls, as those who will give an account. Let them do this with joy and not with grief, for this would be unprofitable for you. Pray for us, for we are sure that we have a good conscience, desiring to conduct ourselves honorably in all things. And I urge you all the more to do this.

Hebrews 13:17–19

Once the governing body of a church or ministry approves screening, introduces it to its members, and selects a screening committee, it is time to begin the actual screening of applicants. There are two parts to the screening process: the primary phase screening, during which present or potential children's ministries workers or volunteers fill out a Children's Ministries Worker Application and submit it for review, and the secondary phase screening, which is used only when questions or concerns arise about an applicant.

The Primary Phase

Ministries find that the majority of applicants have few or no concerns as they pass through the primary phase of screening, because those with potential problems usually decline to be considered for children's ministries once they know they must be screened. Yet even candidates with nothing to hide may be concerned about the information they will be required to provide. The congregation should have been given an opportunity to review and ask questions about the application form (see chapter 2), but it will help if the leader distributing the forms to workers is well acquainted with it. So let us briefly examine the Children's Ministries Worker Application.

The Application Form

The Children's Ministries Worker Application (see appendix 1) is divided into eleven sections. The intent of the application is to weed out potential perpetrators of child abuse. It is a tool to promote safety for families and children, *not* to cause disunity or distrust in a ministry or congregation. Leaders should ensure that screening is handled in such a way that innocent parties know they have nothing to fear.

An overview may help to quell unnecessary concerns regarding the application.

Section 1. This section requests the applicant to provide general information, such as his or her name, address, telephone numbers, occupation, marital status, and church attendance data. It also requests a photograph to accompany the application. In most cases the photograph is simply a formality. However, in screening people who are new in the congregation, it is wise to confirm their identity with a driver's license, passport, or other official photo ID.

Sections 2 and 3. Applicants record ministry positions in which they prefer to serve or are presently serving. (Candidates for the screening committee need only indicate what positions they now hold in section 2 and may skip section 3.)

Section 4. This section asks direct questions about the applicant's criminal record. Although some might find requests for information of this nature offensive, this section must be taken seriously and never be waived. If an applicant has strong objections to the gathering of such information, he or she should pursue a ministry that does not include children.

Sections 5 through 9. These sections ask the applicant to provide a spiritual history from his or her conversion to the present. The main focus of the questions in these sections is the applicant's personal testimony and ministry experiences involving children. (Candidates for the screening committee should not skip sections 7–9. It will be helpful to know what experience and gifts a candidate has since they may be useful in serving on the committee.)

Section 10. Here the applicant is to provide the names of two people who can serve as references, excluding relatives and former employers. These references will verify the applicant's personal and ministry histories. One of these references may be the applicant's pastor.

Section 11. The affirmation and liability waiver must be read and signed by each applicant. If an individual refuses to sign the release, the church runs a major liability risk if that person assumes a children's ministries position. Any applicant who refuses to sign the release should be encouraged to reapply when he or she is ready to sign, or to consider a ministry that does not involve children.

Processing the Application

Once an application is completed, the applicant places it in a sealed envelope and deposits it in a confidential storage container. The best location for this container is a room that is secure and will maintain the integrity and confidentiality of the screening process. The pastor's office can be a good drop off point, because this location ensures that the completed application is not accessible to general church traffic or staff volunteers. One member of the screening committee should be appointed to collect the completed applications on a regular basis.

The screening committee then faces the task of reading through every section of the worker application. It is important that this be done impartially. Neither the applicant's reputation nor that of a reference pastor should cause a screening committee to overlook the details of an application. The reputation of a person cannot justify compromising the integrity of screening.

The screening committee should especially watch for inconsistencies of data, discrepancies of chronologies, changes in marital status, and any past or pending criminal or civil court cases. Particular attention should be paid to those applicants who are recent attendees or newer members.

If a screening committee member expresses concern about a particular response from an applicant or requests further explanation of a section of the application, the committee then begins the secondary phase screening process. Only under extreme circumstances should a screening committee reject an application without first completing the secondary phase. However, if such a rejection occurs, the applicant should receive either a verbal or written communication from the screening committee tactfully explaining the reasons for the rejection. Any verbal communication should be witnessed by at least two members. The committee should communicate with every applicant after each phase of the screening, but it is especially important to communicate promptly and lovingly to anyone whose application is rejected.

The Secondary Phase

Once the applications are returned and the primary phase is complete, the majority of candidates will not need to move to the next step in screening. The secondary phase screening process is an optional deeper level of screening that takes place when

1. clarification is needed concerning an answer given on an application,

2. a reference raises new concerns about the applicant, or
3. it is necessary for the applicant to undergo a formal background check.

As the secondary phase begins, the screening committee should be reminded of its duty to minister to the applicants, whether or not their applications are accepted for ministry. They should also act with tact and love, being sensitive to the possibility that this process might damage the applicant's self-esteem or diminish confidence in his or her gifts or abilities.

Interviewing Applicants

When there is sufficient concern over an application, the screening committee should set up an interview with the applicant. The purpose of the interview should be clearly stated up front, and care should be taken not to frighten or provoke the applicant. The committee members should make sure the applicant understands that their goal is to resolve certain concerns so that he or she can participate in children's ministries, and that the applicant always has the right to withdraw his or her name from consideration.

A simple request for clarification of a written response can be made over the telephone. Such a clarification may be needed if an applicant did not answer a written question clearly or when a reference provided inadequate or conflicting information.

Any more serious concerns necessitate an interview in person with all of the members of the screening committee. In this case, the committee should have a list of questions prepared in advance that cover the applicant's position on discipline, child abuse, and other issues concerning children. The following questions provide a starting point, but each interview will require different questions based on the concerns raised in that particular application.

What types of discipline do you think are appropriate for children? The purpose of this question is to gain insight into the applicant's views on discipline, ranging from verbal reprimands to corporal punishment. Does the applicant understand the important difference between the actions that provoke disciplinary consequences and the person needing discipline? Is the applicant's discipline style compatible with the ministry's position? Does he or she have a rigid disciplinary approach that lacks the flexibility needed in working with children? Or is the applicant so passive or permissive that he or she would be unable to keep control of a classroom? Hypothetical scenarios can be used to ask the applicant's response to particular discipline situations.

What frustrates you most at home, at work, about children, and about society in general? This four-part question probes for the applicant's hot buttons. These are areas about which the applicant is passionate or which he or she cannot control. For example, an uncompromising position that children should be spanked for willful disobedience could make a worker very uncomfortable in a children's ministry program where corporal punishment is not allowed. On the other hand, an individual who expresses resentment toward authority figures may find it difficult to follow ministry policies. The answers to this question are important because there will always be certain children who find and push these hot buttons.

What do you think will be the hardest part of working in children's ministries? This question prompts applicants to examine their motivation for working with children and assess whether there is something in their lives that could hinder their ministry with children. This is an appropriate time to present relevant information from the applicant's references to substantiate possible concerns of the screening committee. Be careful to remain nonjudgmental, because all of us have weaknesses and shortcomings. Identifying these areas should not necessarily disqualify a person from working with children.

How would you define child abuse? Individuals have various definitions of child abuse, which may or may not be accurate.

As a result, it is extremely important to determine what the applicant regards as abuse—physical, sexual, and emotional. Committee members should already know state and federal definitions of child abuse as well as reporting laws (see chapter 5 for further information). Be especially cautious if an applicant is unable to define abuse or has a permissive definition. Perpetrators can delude themselves on what constitutes abuse in an attempt to pacify their conscience.

Background Check

The most serious concerns can only be addressed through an official background check. Some churches and ministries run mandatory background checks, including fingerprinting, on all children's ministries workers. Although a majority do not require them, several church leaders interviewed for this book came to the conclusion that a day is coming in the near future when all church workers, whether volunteer or paid, will be required to submit to mandatory background checks and fingerprinting. A background check becomes imperative when it is the only way to obtain crucial information needed to ensure security for children and ministry programs.

You can obtain a background check through your local police or sheriff's office. The individual being checked must fill out forms and be fingerprinted, and there is usually a nominal fee. Then the law enforcement network checks for any criminal record—both local and national. Since convicted sex offenders are required to register with local authorities, they would not risk exposure by permitting a background check, and so they would remove themselves from consideration.

Usually the church will receive a form letter providing the search results. Although it is hoped that a background check will reveal no cause for concern, it will uncover any criminal problem—from outstanding parking tickets to murder.

If it becomes clear during the interview or background check that a person has been arrested, convicted, or accused of child sexual abuse in the past,[22] then the committee has a responsibility to move quickly and carefully. The committee should report their findings to the senior pastor and governing board, and the ministry's insurance company and lawyer should be notified immediately. They can advise the church as to what constitutes an acceptable risk under the circumstances. Whether the accusations of abuse are in the recent or distant past, it is wise to restrict the individual from access to any children's ministries. But do not react with panic or judgmentalism. See chapter 7 for an in-depth discussion of ministering to accused or convicted perpetrators.

The Decision

At the conclusion of the secondary phase screening, there must be a unanimous decision by the screening committee in order to place a worker into children's ministries. Unanimity is crucial at this point. If any committee members have reservations concerning an applicant, the committee should

1. advise the applicant to wait six months and reapply,
2. encourage him or her to pursue other ministries at the church that do not include children, and/or
3. recommend dismissal of a worker from any present position in children's ministry.

Applicants refused children's ministries positions should be notified in person by at least two members of the screening committee to provide accountability and sufficient witnesses to the conversation. Such cases must be handled delicately and with love. It may be appropriate to enlist the senior pastor and/or someone from the governing body of the church to act as a mediator.

A waiting period of six months is advised for applicants not accepted for a children's ministry position. During this waiting period, the applicant should refrain from working with children, and unless extremely serious concerns exist, he or she could pursue another avenue of ministry not involving children. The screening committee could even suggest several other ministry opportunities for the person to consider. At the end of the six months, the applicant should have the option to submit a new Children's Ministries Worker Application and begin the screening process again.

A Step in the Right Direction

Screening of children's ministries workers does not limit ministry, nor is it a step backward. Instead, screening is a step in the direction of good stewardship. There may be situations in which programs must be closed because of a lack of screened workers, but that does not mean the ministry is a failure. God's work should be done sensibly and with wisdom, and placing children in risky situations is certainly neither sensible nor wise. We do not fail in ministry when we make the safety of children a priority.

Those who believe they have failed if they close down a children's ministry program because of a lack of screened workers need to evaluate the purpose of the program. Ministry leaders must challenge the perception that once a program is under way it should continue perpetually. Some ministries may be only for a season; others may be for several years. God is gracious enough to bring opportunities for ministry expansion, but he would shut down a children's ministry program that is not safe and secure for the little ones.

Part 2

Postscreening Issues

After children's ministries workers have been screened, how can we continue to ensure safety for children? What should a worker do if he or she suspects that one of the children is a victim of abuse? How should a church respond to an accusation of child abuse? What is the church's responsibility in ministering to an accused perpetrator as well as to the victim?

In part 2 we will explore the functioning of a ministry after screening has been put in place. These and other related questions will be answered as we look at additional safeguards, responding to accusations of abuse, and restoration of an abuser to fellowship with believers.

-5-

Safeguards

> You, however, continue in the things you have learned and
> become convinced of, knowing from whom you have learned
> them; and that from childhood you have known the sacred writ-
> ings which are able to give you the wisdom that leads to salva-
> tion through faith which is in Christ Jesus. . . . that the man of
> God may be adequate, equipped for every good work.
>
> 2 Timothy 3:14–15, 17

Implementing a screening ministry does not complete the task of safeguarding our children and families. Having trustworthy workers is essential, but these workers must be supervised and follow guidelines for appropriate behavior when working with children. The time required to establish safety policies and procedures and to properly train workers is time well spent. These safeguards not only provide for the safety of children and the peace of mind of their parents but also protect workers from putting themselves in a compromising position, as the following two stories illustrate.

Church Nursery Allegation. Due to staffing pressures, a well-meaning pastor made an unwise decision to allow a recovering alcoholic, who had been abused as a child, to work in the church nursery. When the child's parents observed her mistreating their little one, they accused her of child sexual abuse. After meeting with both parties, the senior pastor concluded that nothing had happened. However, the worker is undergoing long-term counseling and is no longer permitted access to children's ministries in the church.

This church did not screen its children's ministries workers. A screening ministry might have kept this woman out of the nursery in the first place, but even if she had passed through screening, proper supervision could have minimized her opportunity to act inappropriately, and a clear understanding of church policy on treatment of children could have kept her from even the appearance of abuse.

The Winter Camp Scare. At a winter youth camp, a male youth leader reached out and grabbed the back of a high school girl's knee. The youth leader thought the girl was part of his youth group, but he soon found out the young woman belonged to another youth group that was using the same facility.

The girl went to her leader and complained that this man touched the back of her leg. The girl's leader then demanded a meeting with the leaders of both youth groups. At that meeting, she chastised the male leader for abusive behavior. "How dare you touch one of my girls on her leg? You must have a problem."

There was a long, tense waiting period as the pastoral staff of the male leader's church wondered whether the girl, her leader, or her parents would report the incident as sexual abuse or molestation. Fortunately for the offending youth leader and his church, the girl's parents did not see any need to report the incident.

Although the man was merely being playful and had meant no harm, his actions were easily misinterpreted and could have resulted in a court case. The youth leader and his church could have been spared many anxious moments if the church had established careful guidelines for the behavior of its workers.

Guidelines provide workers with clear definitions of what is and is not appropriate in their interactions with children in the church. Churches should have policies that apply to everyone so workers are not left to make their own decisions on these important and possibly litigious issues.

Along with clear guidelines, involved supervisors can do much to eliminate the possibility of abuse occurring and to ensure that workers are not falsely accused of abuse. Such supervision does not mean that leaders spy on their workers. Instead, leaders should disciple their workers, hold them accountable, and support and encourage them in their ministry.

Worker Supervision

Supervision of children's ministries workers should not be authoritarian but instead should promote trust, accountability, and leader-worker rapport. This can be accomplished through a team-oriented ministry approach in which leaders and workers strive toward the same goal.

One way leaders can promote teamwork is to maintain high visibility, which facilitates communication and builds a sense of teamwork and trust. High visibility also fosters accountability. It is healthy for workers to be responsible to provide quality ministry.

If workers are unsupervised, they minister with a sense of isolation. Yet overly supervised workers may feel trapped in a Big Brother network that questions their motives and actions and promotes a sense of fear rather than trust. Both extremes should be avoided. Workers should not be left on their own, but they also should not be made to feel that someone is constantly peering over their shoulder. Instead, the leader's presence ought to encourage and uplift the workers.

Leaders can also nurture workers through discipleship so that they serve willingly and faithfully. Discipleship in this context facilitates growth in the worker's ministry and personal life. In the context of safety for children, discipleship will promote growth in interpersonal relationships, between the workers themselves as well as between workers and children. Two classic resources in the area of discipleship are J. Oswald Sanders's book, *Spiritual Leadership,* and Francis M. Cosgrove's *Essentials of Discipleship.*[23]

Rescreening will also be the responsibility of children's ministries supervisors. This informational update should take place annually or biannually. Appendix 1 provides a sample Children's Ministries Rescreening Form, which requests any changes in address, marital status, employment, or ministry positions. It also serves as a method of accountability by reminding the worker that safety is still a priority.

Training workers is another task of supervisors. This training occurs on a regular basis through discipleship, but it is crucial to include more formal training that incorporates all children's ministries workers.

Training Workers

Almost every facet of our lives depends on some sort of training, whether employment, athletics, hobbies, driving an automobile, or volunteering on the school council. The church has an obligation to equip those who serve. Children's ministries workers with proper training are more confident and make fewer mistakes. Well-trained workers are also better able to protect children in their care. But training programs are not always popular.

One common criticism of church training sessions is that they are not practical. One person commented, "They give us too much information and do not show us how to use it." Boring material, an irrelevant lecture, or an unplanned agenda can also leave workers feeling that their time was wasted. The training material must be relevant and practical. A seminar lecture for nursery staff on the various philosophies of Christian education is doomed from the start, but most volunteer workers in the primary and intermediate department will be interested in hearing ways to hold the attention of a group of wiggly first graders.

Although we will offer practical information on training children's ministries workers in general, the focus of this book is the safety of children and families, so we will give special attention to reducing the risk of an occurrence of child abuse.

Teacher Training

The church leadership and pastoral staff bear the responsibility to offer necessary training for volunteers, and their support is crucial to the integrity of children's programs. When there is only one pastor, or in ministries in which there is no direct pastoral leadership for children's ministries, it is extremely important to develop layleaders to direct the children's ministries program and train workers. These leaders should provide encouragement, emotional support, and practical assistance for children's ministries workers.

Some pastors may take an active role in children's ministries. Others may show support through recruitment or ministry development. Although such support should be expected, it is wise to have well-defined roles. If both sides strive toward an equitable working relationship, they can avoid pastoral burnout from unrealistic ministry expectations as well as layworker burnout from lack of pastoral support.

Both pastors and workers may be concerned about how much time training will take from their already busy schedules. Training for children's ministry volunteers can take a variety of forms. The types of training used will determine how much time is required. Videos, audio tapes, and printed training materials abound at your local Christian bookstore.[24] If you are able to attend the annual Christian Booksellers Convention (held in a different city each year), you will be able to preview a wealth of excellent materials for training workers. Christian radio stations, newspapers, and colleges may also know of training seminars in the area or be able to provide training resources through their own speakers or programs. National ministries, such as those of Gene Getz, James Dobson, and Jay Adams, also offer trustworthy training programs.[25]

Church leaders and workers can visit other churches to gain valuable insight into the successful elements of other ministries' programs, as long as this is done in the spirit of learning from and supporting each other rather than comparing and competing. Another shared learning opportunity is available through conventions sponsored by regional Sunday school associations or the Association of Christian Schools International (ACSI).[26]

The best format, however, is the church-sponsored seminar. Periodic training seminars are informative and refreshing when they are well planned and use time wisely. Saturday mornings usually work best for training sessions, which should run for only one to two hours. Audio and/or video tapes could be made of the seminar for those who find it impossible to attend.

Rather than focusing on issues of philosophy of ministry or becoming mired in theological issues, training should focus on practical issues such as teaching methods, craft construction, question and answer suggestions, techniques for positive discipline, and ways to deal with the especially difficult child. Some classic works in this area are *Adult Education in the Church*, by Roy B. Zuck, and *A Theology of Christian Education*, by Lawrence O. Richards. Two lively series (video and printed) by Howard Hendricks are *7 Laws of the Teacher* and *7 Laws of the Learner*. Hendricks's snappy, humorous, and straightforward approach is a welcome addition to any training session. Two excellent Christian journals, *Leadership Journal* and *Christian Education Journal*, provide cutting edge suggestions for worker training.[27]

Safety Training

Establish safety procedures before discussing abuse:

Where do the children enter the building for the activity?
What is church policy regarding accompanying children to the rest room?

Is there a sign-in procedure?

Are the children supposed to eat while in our care?

What areas of the facility are off-limits to children?

Some of these questions will have different answers depending on the ages of the children. For that reason, it is wise during part of a training seminar to break up into age-specific groups.

Another practical aid is to acquaint all children's ministries workers with the layout of the ministry facility. Workers benefit more when this includes a walk-through of the facility. This tour could include classrooms, rest rooms, storage rooms, heating and cooling thermostats, fire extinguishers (and instructions on their use), smoke alarms, and the supervisor's and superintendent's offices. All workers should also be made aware of emergency policies such as evacuation routes, procedures for contacting parents in case of injury or illness of a child, injury or accident report forms, clean-up and sanitary procedures for sick children, and so on.

Following is a suggested schedule for a children's ministries training seminar. The program assumes a two-hour session with an accompanying continental breakfast. Churches can improvise on this schedule to meet their unique needs.

Children's Ministries Workers Training Seminar

8:15–8:30 A.M.	Coffee and Continental Breakfast
8:30–8:40 A.M.	Introduction of Children's Ministries Leaders
8:40–9:00 A.M.	General Policies and Procedures of Children's Ministries
9:00–9:30 A.M.	Departmental Break Out Groups
9:30–10:00 A.M.	Exploration of "What If" Scenarios
10:00–10:25 A.M.	Question and Answer Session
10:25–10:30 A.M.	Announcement of Next Training and Dismissal

General policies and procedures of children's ministries. During this segment, distribute and review the church's policies and procedures. Highlight the most important information and point out any changes. To keep things moving and to ensure you will have enough time to cover all the material, don't answer questions at this time. Workers should write down any questions they have and hand them to the seminar leaders to be answered later during the question and answer segment.

Departmental break out groups. Workers break up into groups by departments (nursery, kindergarten through sixth grade, youth) to review the policies and procedures of each department. It may be helpful during this session to conduct a brief tour of the facilities, especially the rooms that will be used by each department. Again, workers should write down questions to be answered in the question and answer segment or at a later departmental meeting.

Exploration of "what if" scenarios. Scenarios should be realistic and pertain to procedures to be followed for fires, evacuation, and other safety matters. This is not a time for workers to suggest "what ifs"; they should be reserved for a departmental meeting held another time.

Question and answer session. To keep things moving during this brief segment, leaders can sort through the questions and provide answers to the most pertinent ones. This method will save time by weeding out irrelevant questions and by keeping anyone from monopolizing the floor. Any concerns and questions unaddressed in the time allotted can be answered in a departmental meeting, in another training seminar, or by publishing the questions and answers in a pamphlet.

Worker training seminars are not intended to provide answers to every question or to cover every possible scenario. Neither are they opportunities for workers to address their pet peeves. Rather these seminars are overviews of general policies and issues. Some churches will be able to cover the most important material in one training seminar; however, this necessitates covering the highlights quickly, avoiding general discussion, and supplying a handbook that provides the details. Other churches will find it easier to cover the information in multiple seminars. This will allow more thorough discussion and more time to answer questions. In such cases, the leaders will need to decide which areas should be covered first and which can be covered in a later seminar.

Safety Policies

Each worker should be given a written list of important policies and procedures before he or she starts working in children's ministries. Each church or ministry will have its own specific guidelines, and they will need to include other areas besides safety procedures. Some of the following suggested guidelines may seem overly cautious, but it is important to remember the priority of ensuring safety for the children to whom we minister. Always keep in mind that the more precautions we take to protect our children, the less we are at risk of a lawsuit.

General Policies (All Ages)

Christian education pastors, Sunday school superintendents, or other leaders should regularly visit classrooms and activities. High visibility of leaders encourages and supports workers while enhancing security for children.

Teachers and workers should display loving attitudes toward the children in their care. Children know when they are loved and appreciated, and this is a vital part of the overall ministry to the families of the church.

Children should receive love, nurture, and protection. Negative remarks about children or parents shall not be tolerated.

Emergency exits should be easily accessible to all children, and all workers should know at least two exit routes.

Nursery (Birth through Preschool)

Some find a rewarding ministry in caring for children from infancy through preschool. Babies and toddlers are easy to love, but this ministry can be especially helpful for tired parents seeking an undistracted hour of worship and serenity.

It is particularly important that nursery workers instill confidence in parents who hand over their infants or preschoolers. These little ones are defenseless, and for that reason, the nursery staff must be carefully chosen—never grabbing the closest warm body. Staffing with last-minute replacements puts great stress upon nursery workers and diminishes parental confidence. A reserve list of qualified substitutes can solve this problem before it occurs.

The following are policies for this age group.

Nursery supervisors should be members of the church.

The crib nursery should be staffed by adult women only.

Nursery workers in the ones to threes rooms should be at least sixteen years old. Any younger helpers should be assistants rather than scheduled workers, and they should not assume responsibility for any of the children.

Younger helpers who have siblings in the nursery should never be expected to serve as the drop-off or pick-up person. The presence of the parents is an added safety feature, because the workers will know they might be observed as they care for the children.

Parents should be welcome in the nursery rooms at any time, especially when their children need their attention.

Children should be signed in and checked out by a parent or another authorized adult. A child should never be released to a person unfamiliar to the nursery staff.[28]

Nurseries should follow the two-adults rule at all times. No adult worker should be alone with any child behind a closed door. Exception can be made only if the worker is the child's parent, when parental permission is given ahead of time, or in case of an emergency.

The two-adults rule also applies to escorting a child into a closed-door rest room. Several children, with at least two adults, should enter the rest room together. The same exceptions can apply here as in the previous case.

Under no circumstances should a children's ministries worker touch a child for the purpose of corporal punishment. Discipline should be handled in a calm, loving manner, beginning with eye contact and expressions of gentle concern, and removing the child from the room only in the most disruptive cases. A child's parents should be asked to come to the nursery as a last resort if the problem persists.

If a child is taken to a more private location for disciplinary measures, there must be two adult workers nearby. An exception can be made if an open door to the hallway or an adjoining room allows complete visibility of the child.

Under no circumstances should a single child or a group of children be left unattended in any room at the church or ministry.

Rooms should be well lit, preferably with windows in the doors for viewing from outside or Dutch doors that can be left open. There should also be no hidden corners, closets, or storage rooms.

Any detached storage cabinets should be anchored to the wall to prevent toppling.

Primary and Intermediate (Kindergarten through Grade Six)

Teachers in the primary through intermediate department have a special opportunity because most of these children are impressionable and, therefore, teachable. They still have a natural curiosity, innocence, and inclination to trust adults. Personalities and attitudes are being forged with each new day. It is at this age that children seem the most open to accepting the truth of Christ's love.

The following are policies for this age group.

Teachers in the primary and intermediate department must be at least eighteen years of age.

Primary and intermediate workers should make every effort to commit to a year-long teaching and/or working relationship with the children. Consistency is a significant factor in nurturing a relationship of trust.

Activities and learning environments should be challenging and fun. Elevating the interest levels of each child cuts down on discipline problems.

Leadership should be highly visible on days when programs are in session. This will give parents opportunities to meet and chat with their ministry leaders. It also frees up the teachers and workers to focus on their tasks rather than field a multitude of questions.

There should be regularly scheduled meetings with parents to introduce new ministry ideas, camps, outings, competitions, etc. These meetings are excellent times to inform the parents of policies, procedures, and guidelines for activities.

No adult worker should be alone with any child behind a closed door unless the worker is that child's parent, parental permission has been obtained, or in case of an emergency.

Children should never be dropped off at a ministry activity unless there is a leader present. Parents should stay with their children until a leader arrives.

Primary and intermediate workers need to be familiar with the person dropping off or picking up a child. If there is any doubt, the child should be kept in the room until the parent or guardian arrives or until parental permission is given.[29]

A single child or group of children should not be left unattended in any room at the church or ministry.

Youth (Junior High through High School)

Youth workers can have a tremendous impact on the lives of many young people. But youth ministry brings unique challenges, which must be taken seriously.

By definition, youth work is with children in their adolescent years, typically between the ages of twelve and eighteen. Adolescents have particular concerns, unlike those of younger children. These young people are experiencing physical and emotional changes that affect the dynamics of youth ministry. Children of this age are no longer susceptible to promises of candy, but they are vulnerable in other ways. Adolescents need affirmation from their peers and others they respect, such as leaders, teachers, and parents. They are also learning to deal with biological responses to members of the opposite sex. These new feelings of passion or love—and sometimes lust—make even a passing crush seem like "the love of my life." Special attention from a person in a leadership role can truly minister to an emotionally needy adolescent, but a predator in a leadership position can easily use a position of power to take advantage of the emotionally vulnerable child. Even if the child seems to want romantic involvement, adults should be aware that sexual activity is still a criminal act.

Churches should establish codes of behavior for their youth leaders and workers to avoid any possibility of sexual abuse. It is wise for each church to publish its own set of specific behavioral guidelines and require all youth leaders and workers to sign it. Some examples of behavioral rules are included with the following policies.

Youth ministry workers should be at least nineteen years of age and be either a high school graduate or out of high school for at least one year.[30]

Youth leaders must be members of the church and have a record of success in other ministries in the church.

Sexual harassment, either active or passive, verbal or nonverbal, is inappropriate among youth leaders, workers, and youth group members.

Dating between youth and leaders or workers is inappropriate. There should be no romantic involvement between youth and workers. Any worker who desires a romantic relationship with any of the youth should be released from his or her position in children's ministry.

Playful or amorous physical contact is to be avoided between leaders, workers, and youth.

Workers should not be alone with youth members of the opposite sex in any room, parked automobiles, residences, etc. Ideally, a leader also should not be alone with a youth of the same sex in order to avoid any suspicion of homosexual abuse. In this age group, the safest ministry is group ministry, which facilitates accountability.

Extra care should be exercised when transporting youth. It is preferable to have at least two leaders per vehicle. But when only one leader is available, the leader and youth members are to refrain from affectionate physical contact (departing hugs or kisses).

Youth leaders and workers should inform someone in authority over them if, during the transportation of youth, there was cause to stop a vehicle (for counseling, discussion, etc.). As soon as possible, the driver should document in writing the events that transpired.

Youth leadership should meet with parents at least once a quarter to announce special activities or new ministry ideas.

These meetings are excellent times to explain the focus of youth ministry and allow parents to meet youth workers.

Overnight activities and out-of-town retreats should be well chaperoned. Each church should ensure that all participants clearly understand behavioral expectations, particularly in regard to members of the opposite sex, and the consequences for breaking the rules.

Leadership should establish guidelines for acceptable and unacceptable physical contact between members of the opposite sex and communicate them clearly to the youth.

Permission Slips

Any time children attend an event sponsored by the church or ministry, liability issues are raised. For that reason, every effort should be made to secure parental or guardian permission for all children who attend ministry-sponsored activities. Implied permission can be assumed as parents drop off their children for on-site programs such as Sunday school classes, midweek children's activities, or any other function where roll sheets are used. However, it is important to require parents to sign in their children as an attendance register and a confirmation that the church received a child into its care. Implied permission may be adequate for the younger children, whose only activities are at the ministry facility, but when children are old enough to participate in off-site trips, camps, or other activities, permission slips become essential.

Many churches have general permission slips that give consent to attend all church-sponsored events. Others require activity-specific permission slips, which specify time of departure, method of transportation, time of return, adults who will be chaperoning, emergency telephone numbers, health insurance information, permission to provide emergency medical treatment, and a waiver of the church's liability for injury. These slips must be signed by a parent or guardian, and leaders should carry them throughout the activity. Some churches allow permission slips to be submitted by fax. In such cases leaders should telephone parents or guardians directly to verify the permission granted. Verbal permission should be the exception rather than the rule, used only in cases in which a young person has forgotten his or her permission slip and only when the verbal permission can be confirmed by a ministry leader.

Child Abuse (Sexual and Physical)

There are various ways to define child sexual abuse, and for that reason it is important that all children's ministries workers be provided a clear definition of abuse according to the laws of their state. This information can be obtained from your state's Child Protective Services (see the listing in appendix 4), and should be supplied to all workers in writing as well as being covered in a training seminar.

For example, the state of Arizona has a five-fold categorization of child abuse, which includes emotional abuse, child neglect, shaken infant syndrome, physical abuse, and sexual abuse. Definitions vary from state to state, but they usually contain similar elements.[31] As a guideline for ministries, the Church Law and Tax Report Office defines child sexual abuse as "criminal behavior that involves children in sexual behaviors for which they are not personally, socially, and developmentally ready," and "any form of sexual contact or exploitation in which a minor is being used for the sexual gratification of the perpetrator."[32] The National Resource Center on Child Sexual Abuse adds that "the abuser may be an adult, an adolescent, or another child, provided the child is four years older than the victim."[33]

Even with a clear definition of child abuse, some may find it difficult to determine which behaviors suggest a child has been abused. Children's ministries workers should not be suspicious of every unusual action, but they should investigate signs that a child has been in a situation that is potentially harmful to his or her physical, emotional, spiritual, or sexual well being. Visible bruises or seemingly irrational fears should call attention to the possibility that the child may be in danger. (See appendix 3 for a list of specific physical and behavioral signs that may indicate a child has been sexually abused.)

When a children's ministries worker suspects that a child has been abused, he or she should immediately report it to the pastoral staff member who oversees the ministry. If there is no pastoral staff member directly in charge, the departmental leader, director, or superintendent should receive the report. This removes the primary responsibility from the shoulders of the volunteer worker. The leader who receives the report is then obligated to check the information and notify the authorities if necessary.

Many states have reporting laws that require any form of child abuse to be reported within one day from the time a person has reason to suspect that the abuse has occurred, and there are some stiff fines for not reporting suspected child abuse within the allotted time. Leaders should check with their state's Child Protective Services to verify the allowable window of child abuse reporting. (See appendix 4 for a state-by-state listing.)

The church's attorney should always be consulted, especially if there is any doubt about whether to report an incident. In addition, the church should contact its insurance representative immediately after reporting suspected abuse to the local authorities. The legal issues should not be downplayed or underestimated when it comes to the issue of child sexual abuse. (See chapter 6 for an in-depth discussion on responding to accusations of abuse within a ministry.)

The legal issues involved make it imperative that ministries and churches hold general meetings with all workers to relate accurate information about reporting abuse. Included on an agenda at such a meeting should be:

Legal definitions of child abuse.

What to do when child abuse of any kind is suspected.

The personal and ministry responsibilities of reporting all forms of child abuse.

The ministry's lawyer and insurance company representative should be asked to attend this meeting and be available to answer questions.

Safeguarding children, families, and ministries is a vital ministry task. Following the suggestions in this book will greatly reduce the risk, but even the best of training, the most prolific lawyer, and the highest level of leader visibility is no absolute guarantee that no abuse of any kind will occur at your facility. It is for that reason that the following chapter addresses how to deal with an allegation of abuse within your church or ministry.

-6-

Response Plans

Be ready in season and out of season; reprove, rebuke, exhort, with great patience and instruction.

2 Timothy 4:2

By properly screening, training, and supervising children's ministries workers, we seek to avoid an incident of child sexual abuse in our church or ministry. However, it is important to have a well-defined response plan to implement if such an unfortunate event should nevertheless occur. By writing a plan ahead of time, ministries can determine before an incident occurs what appropriate steps should be taken in response, thus avoiding the damaging mistakes that can result from the frustration, anger, or hysteria often brought on by accusations and lawsuits. The guidelines in this chapter will help you form a legal, ethical, and Christian response to an allegation of child sexual abuse in your ministry.

Obtaining Information

When an incident of child abuse of any kind is reported to a church or ministry leader, remove the accused worker from any active ministry service until an investigation can be completed. This is not to assume guilt but rather to protect the ministry from further liability.

Because of reporting laws for child abuse (see chapter 5), an informal investigative interview should be scheduled immediately. There should be at least three interviewers, including the senior pastor or ministry director and members of the leadership staff. The interviewers should take these five basic steps:

1. Interviewers set out to *acquire* information regarding the alleged incident.
2. Interviewers are to take the *alleged* incident seriously and investigate it impartially.
3. Interviewers are to *affirm* to the parties involved that their goal is to search for the truth of the situation.
4. Interviewers should *assure* the parties that their confidentiality will be guarded.
5. Interviewers then report to the ministry leadership, who must *assess* the information gathered and determine whether to report the incident to the authorities.

The victim and alleged abuser should be interviewed separately, and a child should never be interviewed alone; at least one parent or guardian must be present. Each interview should be carefully recorded, with one or two interviewers appointed as secretaries or using a tape recorder to document the testimony.

Extreme care should be exercised in cases when children have accused their parents of abuse. Although these situations are delicate, the church or ministry has the same legal responsibility as well as an ethical obligation to take action to protect children, even if the abuse did not occur at a ministry function. The child should be allowed to choose the nonoffending parent or some other trusted adult to be with him or her during the interview. When cases such as these arise, churches should immediately seek advice from an attorney.

During the investigative interview, all of the church staff, not just the interviewers, should not take sides. They must be careful to support all individuals involved, being sensitive to the potentially damaged reputation of the accused, as well as the need to ensure the safety of other children.

Interviews with children should be handled with great care to avoid causing further harm to an already injured child. Most children will feel anxious being interviewed by a group of adults. The interviewers need to create a nurturing, non-threatening atmosphere. The adults should keep their tone of voice and line of questioning supportive of the child at all times, while being careful not to suggest things to the child that later might be interpreted as leading the witness and invalidate the child's testimony.

The interview should not be the place for insults or confrontations. Instead the focus of the interviewers should be on finding the truth and determining whether there is enough evidence to report an incident of child sexual abuse to the local authorities. To this end, interviewers must be patient and calm in order to gain the confidence of the parties involved and assure each that their promise of confidentiality will not be broken. However, it must also be made clear that once the authorities become involved, the investigation may become part of public record. The victim's family should be allowed to choose to engage their own attorney to act as their spokesperson or to use the church for that role.

After the interviews have been conducted, one of three conclusions may be reached:

1. There is nothing to the allegation.
2. There is a possibility that the child was abused, but there are still uncertainties.
3. There are enough facts to determine that abuse occurred.

In any of these cases, the ministry leadership should contact their attorney, the insurance company agent, and a Child Protective Services representative. Even if the allegation seems false, these people should be consulted for advice.

It is also wise to bring in a Christian counselor to help the victim and his or her family. This can be particularly important if they do not want to contact the authorities about the abuse. Since the church is legally obligated to report suspected abuse, the counselor may be able to help the victim keep control of his or her life by choosing to go to the authorities as well as saving other potential victims from abuse. An experienced counselor can also help the victim and the family retain control of their lives as they move through the stages of pain, guilt, and fear associated with abuse.

In cases of false accusations made out of vindictiveness or hatred or as a prank, professional counseling should be sought for the accuser because false accusations may be a symptom of deep-seated emotional problems. It will be difficult for a falsely accused individual not to harbor ill feelings toward the accuser in cases like these. Confidentiality is a key issue here because if the investigation has been kept secret, less harm will have been done to innocent parties.

Going Public

Once a ministry determines that the local authorities are to be brought in to handle a reported incident of abuse, the response plan is sure to be tested. After the authorities are informed, the incident will almost certainly be made public and the ministry opened to scrutiny. Most American communities treat allegations of child sexual abuse with little or no confidentiality and objectivity. Many will be stunned at the reports, and although the element of shock cannot be minimized, the way a ministry handles the situation will greatly affect its reputation. If the ministry staff cooperates completely with the legal agencies and makes it clear that it has nothing to hide, it takes an important first step toward rebuilding a shattered reputation.

Once the local authorities begin a formal investigation, the ministry staff is no longer in charge. However, the ministry still has a vital role in providing information for the investigation and in supporting both the victim and the abuser with the goal of eventual restoration.

Allegations of child sexual abuse virtually always bring a barrage of media attention. Whether a ministry has developed an adequate response plan may determine the media's coverage—creating scandalous headlines or bringing healing to the community. If a church is viewed as withholding evidence or covering up the truth, it can be assured of bad press at this critical time. Television crews and reporters will show up at the church steps and at the pastor's home. They may even camp out at the homes of ministry leaders or other church members. Unprepared spokespeople may have their words twisted, misrepresented, or taken out of context. Reputations can be damaged beyond repair, and the ministry of the church can be severely impaired.

A ministry can alleviate some of the panic accompanying media attention by preparing for it. A spokesperson should be chosen to handle all public statements. This spokesperson should be a respected church leader who can present information in a compassionate yet calm way. The spokesperson might be the senior pastor, president, or director of the ministry. It is also wise to develop a spokesperson's line of succession in case the appointed person is not available to serve because he or she is a relative of the accused or the victim, is too emotionally attached to the case, or for any reason feels uncomfortable in the role of spokesperson.

Any public announcement should be read from a prepared statement that has been approved by the ministry's attorney. Copies of the statement should be given to the media to ensure accuracy in reporting. In preparing an official statement, it is important to include the following points:

An allegation of child sexual abuse has been made; child sexual abuse is not tolerated by the church.

The incident has been reported to the proper authorities and is being investigated.

The church will do everything it can to cooperate with the investigation.

Due to the safety and privacy of the victim(s) and the perpetrator, names will not be given.

The responsibility of the church is toward healing and restoration of the parties involved.[34]

The following is a sample official written statement.

Good afternoon. My name is _____ (spokesperson). I serve as the ministry spokesperson for the _____ (church or ministry name). I have a prepared statement to read to you at this time.

We, the _____ (church or ministry governing board) of the _____ (church or ministry name) confirm that an allegation of child sexual abuse occurred at our church (or ministry). We neither condone nor tolerate abuse of any kind, and we have reported the incident to the proper authorities. The matter is now being formally investigated. We expect to cooperate with the investigation completely to the best of our ability.

It is incumbent upon us to assist in the safety and protection of the victim(s), while at the same time not to hinder the investigation. As a result of these concerns and out of compassion, we will not release the names of any of the parties involved in the incident.

In closing, we affirm that it is the ministry purpose of the _____ (church or ministry name) to promote healing and wholeness for those involved in this incident. We will pray and work toward this end.

Thank you. We will answer no questions at this time.

_____ (church or ministry governing board)

A straightforward approach with the media from the outset will minimize doubt and skepticism in a community. The ministry should state the numbers of known victims but should avoid speculating as to whether there are other victims. Admitting that there has been an allegation or incident of abuse will not cause additional harm to the ministry, because the truth will come out with or without the church's cooperation. Honesty and sincerity are the best hope for redeeming the ministry's reputation in the eyes of the community.

It is also important to affirm that the proper authorities are handling the case. The ministry's prepared statement can name the official agencies. With its attorney's approval, a ministry may also outline the manner by which the incident was first reported and the actions taken in response.

Cooperation with authorities is one tangible way the ministry can support the abused parties. Such cooperation should be done in consultation with the ministry's legal counsel, which can help determine what information is necessary to develop a case against the alleged perpetrator. This decision will include consideration of issues such as confidentiality, clergy-counselee privilege, safety for other children, and compliance with the law. As always, it is wiser to err on the side of protecting other children and families from similar situations.

Under no circumstances should the church volunteer the identity of any victim, perpetrator, or family member. Investigative reporting and grapevine news will no doubt uncover the names eventually, or at some point the family of the victim might feel compelled to step forward. But this decision is theirs to make, and the ministry should respect the privacy of the injured parties.

The more honest and sincere a ministry is while still respecting the privacy of those involved, the more openness there will be eventually to move toward healing. The church has the responsibility to minister to the injured and bring them back to a healthy relationship in Jesus Christ. True ministry requires movement toward healing and restoration, the topic of the final chapter of this book.

Responding to the Congregation

The ministry spokesperson or senior pastor should also inform the congregation of the incident both verbally and in writing. Included with the statement should be a reiteration of the ministry's policies regarding child abuse. This is vital to show that the incident will in no way be minimized. As before, words must be chosen carefully and delivered tactfully and with wisdom to guard against overreaction or hysteria. However, even with the most cautious approach, it is inevitable that people will wonder whether their child was also a victim.[35]

The congregation should be aware that members of the media might appear at one or more of its services to gather information. Besides quoting the statement given to the media, the report to the corporate body should stress the necessity for confidentiality and safety of the victim(s) and alleged perpetrator as a priority for the church.

The spokesperson or pastor must also request that every effort be made to route all queries and concerns of the congregation through the church or ministry leadership. This can be facilitated by holding a congregational meeting to address questions and concerns. It is important that the meeting have a respected and insightful moderator who is strong enough to guide the session away from a free-for-all or a venting of anger. The moderator should state clearly what is and what is not permissible to discuss.

In a congregational meeting, there will be members who bring up rumors they have heard. Some may question the abilities of the ministry leadership. Others may express fear that the problem is more widespread than has been revealed. There may even be shouted insults. Through all this, the moderator must remain calm and clearly communicate accurate and essential information. Patience and self-control, combined with truly listening to the concerns and fears of the congregation, will be the best way to keep a bad situation from becoming worse.

The goal of the moderator should be to take a possibly volatile situation and move it in the direction of a ministry-focused group of Christians seeking to offer love, support, and even forgiveness. This is a difficult task, but through prayer and proper planning, the most difficult situations can still bring glory to God.

-7-

Restoration

My brethren, if any among you strays from the truth, and one turns him back, let him know that he who turns a sinner from the error of his way will save his soul from death, and will cover a multitude of sins.

James 5:19–20

When child sexual abuse occurs in the church, the reputation of the Lord and his people is tarnished, and many people are hurt in the process—the victims, their families, the family of the perpetrator, others who had trusted the perpetrator, and the church body as a whole. Rebuilding the lives shattered by abuse begins by focusing on three primary concerns: (1) healing of the lives of the victims, (2) repentance, reparation, and eventual restoration of the perpetrator, and (3) rebuilding of trust and oneness in the church community.

Ministering to Victims of Abuse

Sexual abuse robs children of their innocence and can leave them deeply scarred. There is no simple solution to a problem of such magnitude. God in his grace can restore the lost child-like innocence instantly, but in most cases he brings healing over time. The church ought to minister to the victims and their families by showing genuine love as well as providing long-term counseling and support. However, care should be taken that the words and actions of those ministering to the abused do not exacerbate the harm already done. Patience and unconditional love are required to help the victim rebuild the image of a loving, caring, and protective God, an image which may have been distorted or destroyed by the abuser.

Through therapy, loving families, counselors who know what biblical principles to apply, church support groups, and commitment to God's love and acceptance, many families can—and have—overcome the tragedies associated with child sexual abuse. Victims can do all things through Jesus Christ who strengthens them (see Phil. 4:13). The church should lead the way and commit itself to provide the means to such victorious living.

If a church is large enough to support its own Christian counselor as part of the church's ministry, this is the logical place to refer victims for therapy. This counselor should be able to give quality biblical counsel, coupled with long-term care and compassion provided through church support groups. However, most churches are not equipped to handle a regular counseling load. A pastor should not undertake to counsel the victim(s) unless he or she has special training in counseling sexual abuse victims and is comfortable talking about sexuality. Instead, long-term counseling should be referred to local therapists or counseling organizations.[36]

Although individual counseling is imperative, a support group can be of great assistance in the healing process. Churches that are willing to sponsor support groups for survivors of abuse will discover a crucial new ministry. Today, survivors are no longer as afraid to talk about sexual abuse as they were in the past, and it may be enlightening to see how many hidden survivors there are in the church community. Survivor support groups can give empathetic help to young victims in the healing and rebuilding process.

Members of the church community can help or hinder the victim's healing by their attitudes and actions. Some may feel uncomfortable around the victim of abuse. Others may view the victim as damaged goods or as inferior because of the abuse. Such attitudes will continue to victimize the child. Instead, the congregation needs to reach out in love and acceptance, realizing the child needs time to heal.

Restoring the Perpetrator

Loving the sinner and hating the sin is a principle by which the corporate body of Jesus Christ hopes to operate. Nothing will challenge this principle like an incident of child sexual abuse. Steps toward healing begin when God's people view the perpetrator as a sinner for whom Christ died and not define him by his sin.

Although abhorrent, child sexual abuse is not the unpardonable sin. God's unconditional love extends restoration to the perpetrator as well as the victim, and his grace covers a multitude of sins (see James 5:20). While we make every effort to grasp this truth, we may often wonder how God can forgive someone for sexually abusing a child.

We know Jesus said, "Whoever causes one of these little ones who believe in me to stumble, it is better for him that a heavy millstone be hung around his neck, and that he be drowned in the depth of the sea" (Matt. 18:6). But he also said, "If you do not forgive men, then your Father will not forgive your transgressions" (Matt. 6:15). Can the church afford to forgive selectively? Should Christians compare sins to decide which are worse?

Appropriate Forgiveness

Two sections of the New Testament will help us better understand Jesus' perspective. In John 8 the scribes and Pharisees brought to Jesus a woman caught in adultery. Mosaic law allowed them to stone her to death, but Jesus challenged their moral codes by saying, "He who is without sin among you, let him be the first to throw a stone at her" (John 8:7). All the men dropped their stones and left. Rather than condemning the woman, Jesus sent her away with the admonition, "From now on sin no more" (John 8:11).

Some may ask, "Isn't child sexual abuse worse than adultery because an innocent child is victimized? At least adultery involves two consenting adults." The answer may be yes, but that does not give the church the right to define what is forgivable and what is not. Sin is a universal problem, yet God offers forgiveness to all sinners.

In the second section, Jesus warns us against being judgmental. "Do not judge lest you be judged. For in the way you judge, you will be judged; and by your standard of measure, it will be measured to you. And why do you look at the speck that is in your brother's eye, but do not notice the log that is in your own eye?" (Matt. 7:1–3). We may be so busy judging others that we ignore our own sin.

The Scriptures state clearly that we are all sinners: "For all have sinned and fall short of the glory of God" (Rom. 3:23). Even as Christians, we are still tempted to sin. The apostle Paul writes:

> For that which I am doing, I do not understand; for I am not practicing what I would like to do, but I am doing the very thing I hate. But if I do the very thing I do not wish to do, I agree with the Law, confessing that it is good. . . . For the good that I wish, I do not do; but I practice the very evil that I do not wish. . . . I find then the principle that evil is present in me, the one who wishes to do good.
>
> Romans 7:15–16, 19, 21

We must grapple with sin daily. But forgiveness is always available through Christ. "But God demonstrates His own love toward us, in that while we were yet sinners, Christ died for us" (Rom. 5:8). We are all sinners saved by grace. "For by grace you have been saved through faith; and that not of yourselves, it is the gift of God" (Eph. 2:8). When truly repentant, even a child sexual abuse perpetrator can be restored to right standing and fellowship with God.

Believers are called to maintain a life of forgiveness. The apostle James writes, "Therefore, to one who knows the right thing to do, and does not do it, to him it is sin" (James 4:17). Forgiveness and restoration are the right things to do with regard to sin. The ministry of the church is the restoration of fallen brethren. The church must practice forgiveness if restoration is to occur. "But if you do not forgive men, then your Father will not forgive your transgressions" (Matt. 6:15). Truly, the first act of restoration is forgiveness.

Repentance and Accountability

When an offender repents, the church bears the responsibility to work with him or her with the goal of restoration to fellowship.[37] Galatians 6:1 contains a key principle for Christians: "Brethren, even if a man is caught in any trespass, you who are spiritual, restore such a one in a spirit of gentleness; each one looking to yourself, lest you too be tempted." What evidence of repentance should the church look for in the life of the sexual offender? Repentance can be defined as "that inward change of mind, affections, convictions and commitment, rooted in the fear of God and sorrow for the offenses committed against him, which, when accompanied by faith in Jesus Christ, results in an outward turning from sin to God and his service in all of life."[38]

The church's move toward restoration of the offender should require accountability in many areas. True repentance will be manifest in a change in behaviors and habits. The apostle Paul writes, "Do not be deceived, God is not mocked; for whatever a man sows, this he will also reap. For the one who sows to his own flesh shall from the flesh reap corruption, but the one who sows to the Spirit shall from the Spirit reap eternal life" (Gal. 6:7–8).

Believers are to be on guard; habitual sin is not easily eradicated. Old behaviors and habits are difficult to break. Recovery can be even more complicated if the offender has a personality disorder or if he or she was also abused during childhood. It will take much more than a simple apology to bring a permanent change. Some abusers are even sexual addicts who must have long-term therapy and commitment to a support group to live a life of recovery.[39]

Grace and forgiveness are never reasons to continue practicing sin (see Rom. 6:15). Grace should not be an excuse to thrust a child sexual abuse perpetrator into active fellowship too quickly. When can restoration to fellowship be achieved? How long should a church wait to be assured of genuine repentance? The following steps provide a practical guide for churches and ministries as they struggle to answer these and other important questions.

Step 1: Removal from Ministry

The moment an accusation of child abuse of any kind occurs in a ministry, the accused should be immediately removed from any ministry position. This should be followed by interviews to determine the validity of the allegation and whether to contact the local authorities (see chapter 6). Each ministry must decide whether the situation requires formal removal from fellowship and the length of time before restoration can occur.

Step 2: Repentance in Words

A truly repentant perpetrator should give a detailed, public confession. He or she must provide the identities of all victims in the ministry, the time span of the abuse, and any other abuse in which he or she has been involved. The church should be on guard for "a shallow repentance,"[40] which may be a surface feeling of remorse but not a true desire to change. Be especially careful of this with a repeat child sexual abuser who may have cried similar tears of remorse in the past.

Refusal to repent can manifest itself actively, through denial of an incident or retraction of a confession. Or a refusal can be passive, through claiming abuse in his or her own childhood as an excuse or blaming the victim for being seductive. Such rationalizations do not show genuine repentance. Some Christians blame Satan or his demons for child sexual abuse. While Satan is certainly the instigator of such sinful behavior, overemphasis on blaming him may inappropriately remove the perpetrator from his or her responsibility for the abuse.

So how can we know when repentance is real? What must the abuser do to show real contrition? The following guidelines are good indicators of true repentance.

1. The perpetrator must declare that his or her actions were indeed abusive.
2. There must be an openness and willingness to undergo church discipline—even publicly if necessary.
3. A heartfelt and honest confession must be presented without any denial, passing blame, or minimizing of the abuse.
4. The perpetrator must agree to seek and submit to regular, ongoing professional help and to be held accountable by the church.

Step 3: Repentance by Actions

It is vital that the perpetrator cooperate fully in being accountable to local authorities, Christian counseling, and church disciplinary measures. These actions witness to a continuing spirit of repentance on the part of the perpetrator. The church should require mandatory attendance at counseling sessions and adult accountability and support groups as well as regular spiritual mentoring by a mature adult (of the same sex as the perpetrator) in the church. These measures ought to be imposed for a minimum of two years, with the option of an extension if there is not a clear change in the person's life.

Restoration to Fellowship

When a person is arrested for child sexual abuse, the law determines the punishment. The church is not a penal institution; it is the agency for love, discipline, restoration, and healing. Imprisonment of a perpetrator keeps him or her from harming others; however, incarceration does little to minister to the person—this is the responsibility of the church.

Whether or not the abuser serves a jail sentence, the church's goal should be his or her eventual restoration to fellowship. For a period of a year or more, the perpetrator should not attend church functions. Instead, the church leaders or counselors should go to him or her. This time of separation allows the church community time to deal with its anger and reestablish feelings of confidence and safety, and also gives the perpetrator time to go through the process of confession and healing.

The word *restoration* may frighten some into thinking a child sexual abuse perpetrator will again be placed into ministry with children. This is not the intention. Restoration to fellowship is forgiveness at its best. Some church or community members may never come to terms with a church that forgives and restores a sexual abuse perpetrator. However, the church must never forget where each of its members would be without the transforming power of Christ's forgiveness. We are all sinners saved by grace.

Restoration to a ministry other than children's ministry may occur later, but it must be done cautiously and with safety and prevention as priorities. Bill Anderson, a pastor who guided his church through the aftermath of child sexual abuse, writes: "An offender who has repented and has been restored should, at some point, be restored to service after an appropriate period. However, when deciding on the particular place of service, consider the gifts and talents of the person but give high priority to the safety of the children, the confidence of parents, and the integrity of your church."[41]

Due to the nature of the perpetrator's offense, he or she must *never again be allowed access to children's ministries programs or activities.* Even if there has been true repentance and forgiveness, the risk is far too great for the families and children of the church. The reputation of the church should not be tarnished again by placing a known child sexual abuser in a place of temptation. Such negligence should not exist in the Lord's work.

Rebuilding Trust and Oneness

A child sexual abuse incident in the church can cause so much pain in the body of Christ that we might wish we could step back in time and erase sinful actions. But all we can do is move forward through such a difficult experience. Some will move ahead faster than others. The key, however, is that progress is made.

Victims of sexual abuse, whether children or adults, should sense that the church is contending for their well being. Halting the effects of child abuse in ministry may be difficult, but it is not impossible if the church is willing to make this issue a priority. After an incident of abuse has occurred, there are many practical ways that a church can support victims and their families. Some of these are included in the following list.

Offer retraining sessions for children's ministries workers to address safety issues, what went wrong, and how to better protect children in the future.

Encourage families to address issues of child safety in their home.

Offer elective Sunday school classes to instruct parents how to teach their children the difference between good touch and bad touch as well as making them aware of the signs of child abuse (see appendix 3).

Form survivor support groups to assist in rebuilding injured lives.

Use sermons to rebuild confidence in the church's ministries, particularly programs for children.

Choose a Sunday to honor children's ministries workers.

Publish weekly or monthly articles in church flyers addressing the importance of overall church ministry.

Reemphasize screening procedures in the church, including a reevaluation of the present program.

Pray fervently for God to work in the lives of the people in the church and for his intervention in the message that the congregation and outside community receive about this issue.

Listen to those who suggest additional ways to support victims of child sexual abuse.

These positive steps help to safeguard overall church ministry and reinstate a sense of security for families and children's ministries. These steps can also help reestablish the confidence of church members and the local community as the church shows it is serious about eliminating even the remotest possibility of child sexual abuse ever happening again.

Difficult as it may be, offering forgiveness and support to all parties is crucial to the healing of the church and the restoration of trust and oneness in the community of believers. This process of restoration is lengthy. For the perpetrator, it necessitates extensive counseling and accountability. For the victims of abuse, it may require a lifetime of personal healing, self-esteem building, and development of trust, because their innocence has been stolen and relationships with loved ones and possibly even with God have been injured. The church body may feel overwhelmed by the challenges, but it is an important part of Christian ministry to bring restoration to all parties.

Special attention should be given to the restoration needs of the victims and their families. Through prayer, love, and patience, the church may help these survivors of abuse find the ultimate restoration as God's grace returns to them the joy of their salvation (see Ps. 51:10–12).

Restoration for victims of abuse, whether children or adults, necessitates protection from additional harm. Safety must remain the highest concern. Whether sexual abuse has happened in your ministry or if you consider your ministry safeguarded from such occurrences, the call resounds: It should never happen here! May this affirmation never be compromised.

Appendix 1

Children's Ministries Worker Application and Rescreening Form

Children's Ministries Worker Application

The desire of our church is to provide the safest and most secure environment for the children entrusted to our ministry. Consequently, we maintain a children's ministries worker screening ministry. Anyone presently working in any children's ministry, wishing to become a children's ministries worker, or anticipating future children's ministries work is subject to screening. Thank you for your cooperation.

1. Name _____ Date of Birth _____

Please attach a recent photo.

Address _____

    Street   *City*   *State*   *Zip*

Telephone (Home) _____ (Work) _____

Occupation _____ Employer _____

Driver's License Number _____ Social Security Number _____

Marital Status: ___ Single ___ Married ___ Divorced ___ Widowed ___ Remarried

Membership Status: ___ Active Member ___ Regular Attendee ___ Other

2. Please indicate the children's ministries position(s) you are now working in by writing a (1) in the corresponding blank. Indicate the position(s) you prefer to work in with a (2).

___ Christian Education Director

___ Sunday School Teacher

___ Sunday School Substitute

___ Sunday School Classroom Helper

___ Nursery Leader / Worker

___ Baby-Sitter for Special Programs

___ Junior High Youth Leader / Helper

___ Senior High Youth Leader / Helper

___ Seasonal Camp Leader / Counselor

___ Children's Choir, Drama, etc.

___ Other _____

3. Please indicate which age group you wish to work with. If more than one, rank by preference (1 = first choice, 2 = second choice, etc).

___ Infant Nursery
   (Birth—1 yr.)

___ Toddler Nursery
   (1—2 yr.)

___ Early Childhood
   (2—4 yr.)

___ Kindergarten—3rd Grade
   (5—9 yr.)

___ 4th—6th Grade
   (9—12 yr.)

___ Jr.—Sr. High
   (12—18 yr.)

4. Have you ever been arrested for, convicted of, or pleaded guilty to a crime?

      _____ Yes   _____ No

If yes, please explain below.

5. List the names and addresses of churches you attended regularly over the last seven (7) years.

6. Write a brief account of how you became a Christian.

7. List any children's ministries experience you've had over the past seven (7) years.

8. List any nonchurch experience you've had involving children over the past seven (7) years.

9. List any gifts, training, education, or other qualifications that have prepared you for children's ministries work.

10. List two (2) people (not relatives or former employers) who may be contacted as personal references.

1. _____
   Name   *Phone Number*

   _____
   Street   *City*   *State*   *Zip*

2. _____
   Name   *Phone Number*

   _____
   Street   *City*   *State*   *Zip*

Affirmation and Waiver

I affirm that, to the best of my knowledge, the information on this application is correct. I authorize any reference, organization, or church listed on this application to supply any information (including opinions) that may pertain to my character and fitness to work with children.

Regarding the information gathered pertaining to me, I release any individual, organization, church, or ministry from any and all liability for damages that may result to me or my family. In order to ensure confidentiality, I waive any right to inspect any information provided about me by any person or organization.

Should my application be accepted, I agree to be bound by the church or ministry constitution, bylaws, etc., and to refrain from unscriptural conduct in the performance of my services and with children.

I have carefully read this affirmation and waiver. I understand its contents, and I sign it freely.

_____   _____
        Applicant's Signature   *Date*

For Office Use Only *Reference Checks and Interviews*

Reference: _____ Date: _____ Position: _____

Comments:

Reference: _____ Date: _____ Position: _____

Comments:

Interview: _____ Date: _____ Interview By: _____

Comments:

Children's Ministries Rescreening Form

The desire of our church is to provide the safest and most secure environment for the children entrusted to our ministry. Consequently, anyone working in any children's ministry is subject to periodic rescreening so that we may be aware of any changes in address, marital status, employment, or ministry positions. Thank you for your cooperation.

1. Name _____   Social Security Number _____

2. Has your address changed within the last three (3) years? ____ Yes ____ No

   New address: _____

3. Marital status:
   ___ Single
   ___ Married
   ___ Divorced
   ___ Remarried
   ___ Widowed

4. Check all of the children's ministries positions in which you served over the past three (3) years.

   ___ Christian Education
   ___ Sunday School Teacher
   ___ Sunday School Substitute
   ___ Sunday School Classroom Helper
   ___ Nursery Leader / Worker

   ___ Baby-Sitter for Special Programs
   ___ Junior High Youth Leader / Helper
   ___ Senior High Youth Leader / Helper

   ___ Seasonal Camp Leader / Counselor
   ___ Children's Choir, Drama, etc.
   ___ Other _____

5. Has an accusation or allegation of child abuse ever been brought against you? ___ Yes ___ No

6. Has your employer changed within the last three (3) years? ___ Yes ___ No

New employer's name and telephone number: _____

I understand that my signature below affirms my desire to continue serving in children's ministries, and that I agree to be bound by the constitution, bylaws, etc., of the church or ministry. Furthermore, I agree to refrain from unscriptural conduct in the performance of my services in children's ministries.

_____   _____
Applicant's Signature   *Date*

Appendix 2

Principles for the Church

Principle 1

We are to exercise every caution so that no person or experience will lead a believer away from a healthy relationship with Jesus.

One of the more common questions comes in the form of a subtle objection: Why is there a need for children's ministries screening? Usually this question is because of a lack of knowledge regarding the problems associated with abuse.

> At that time the disciples came to Jesus, saying, "Who then is greatest in the kingdom of heaven?" And He called a child to Himself and set him before them, and said, "Truly I say to you, unless you are converted and become like children, you shall not enter the kingdom of heaven. Whoever then humbles himself as this child, he is the greatest in the kingdom of heaven. And whoever receives one such child in My name receives Me; but whoever causes one of these little ones who believe in Me to stumble, it is better for him that a heavy millstone be hung around his neck, and that he be drowned in the depth of the sea."
>
> Matthew 18:1–6

Principle 2

The church should take the higher road in its dealings with people and not respond to each other as the world responds.

Believers are chosen or set apart by God for holy living—the "called out ones." Because our lives are based on scriptural teachings and principles for everyday living, we must deal with sin differently than does the world.

> But we request of you, brethren, that you appreciate those who diligently labor among you, and have charge over you in the Lord and give you instruction, and that you esteem them very highly in love because of their work. Live in peace with one another. And we urge you, brethren, admonish the unruly, encourage the fainthearted, help the weak, be patient with all men. See that no one repays another with evil for evil, but always seek after that which is good for one another and for all men.
>
> 1 Thessalonians 5:12–15

Principle 3

When the church has to work through a problem such as child sexual abuse, it should seek wisdom from above and have as its goal the pursuit of peace.

There are many problems that confront the church. Possibly, your church is now facing its first test in the area of child sexual abuse. Believers often are able to handle these problems by leaning on wisdom gained through experience. However, God and his Word must be the primary source of wisdom in dealing with such matters.

> But the wisdom from above is first pure, then peaceable, gentle, reasonable, full of mercy and good fruits, unwavering, without hypocrisy. And the seed whose fruit is righteousness is sown in peace by those who make peace.
>
> James 3:17–18

Principle 4

Because God forgives a believer's sin, we ought to forgive others when they sin against us.

Sometimes it is difficult to forgive, but we must remember that Christ's death paid the price for us and cleansed us from sin. May we never forget that we all sin and are in need of God's forgiveness.

> Therefore I say to you, any sin and blasphemy shall be forgiven.
> . . . And whosoever shall speak a word against the Son of Man,
> it shall be forgiven him.
>
> Matthew 12:31–32

Principle 5

When any person has knowledge of right and wrong, it is sinful for the person to act knowingly against what is right.

This principle is a check for all believers. We must readjust our thinking and motivations and challenge any preconceived notions on issues. Understanding of the right thing to do often is at odds with our will to do something less.

> Therefore, to one who knows the right thing to do, and does not do it, to him it is sin.
>
> James 4:17

Principle 6

God's people work together with him to solve problems so that their efforts will not be wasted and the overall ministry and integrity of the church will not be discredited.

The preservation of unity among God's people is a high priority. Divisive issues should not drive people apart. Rather, these issues should drive them together, as a team toward God, unified to seek solutions.

> And working together with Him, we also urge you not to receive the grace of God in vain . . . giving no cause for offense in anything, in order that the ministry be not discredited.
>
> 2 Corinthians 6:1, 3

Principle 7

The goal for Christians, regardless of circumstances, is peace.
Church discipline cases are not easy to handle. Each and every situation that requires a form of church discipline must be committed to prayer. For churches facing such difficult situations, it is good to be reminded of the prayerful words of the apostle Paul:

> Now may the Lord of peace Himself continually grant you peace in every circumstance. The Lord be with you all!
>
> 2 Thessalonians 3:16

Principle 8

Spiritually wise Christians should be the ones dealing with those who are found to be in sin.
The church is called to minister. Part of its ministry is the restoration of those who have fallen away from the faith, by actions, lifestyle, and so on. Mature Christians are encouraged to seek out those who are in need of restoration and walk with them as they return to Christ.

> Brethren, even if a man is caught in any trespass, you who are spiritual, restore such a one in a spirit of gentleness; each one looking to yourself, lest you too be tempted. Bear one another's burdens, and thus fulfill the law of Christ.
>
> Galatians 6:1–2

Principle 9

The goal of effective church discipline should be restoration in love.
Unconditional love requires putting aside the natural feelings of resentment. Loving those who are either in the process of being disciplined by the church or have already been disciplined

can be difficult. It is often easier to avoid the sinner rather than follow the Lord's call for the church to forgive people and reaffirm God's love. Love approaches a fallen brother or sister with unconditional commitment toward restoration to fellowship with God and the church.

> But if any has caused sorrow, he has caused sorrow not to me. . . . Sufficient for such a one is this punishment which was inflicted by the majority, so that on the contrary you should rather forgive and comfort him, lest somehow such a one be overwhelmed by excessive sorrow. Wherefore I urge you to reaffirm your love for him.
>
> 2 Corinthians 2:5–8

Principle 10

The Christian who is willfully practicing sin is to be removed from fellowship and service in the church.

Where do Christians draw the line with unrepentant offenders who have willfully walked away from biblical morality or their profession of faith? The apostle Paul gives us insight into this concern.

> But actually, I wrote to you not to associate with any so-called brother if he should be an immoral person, or covetous, or an idolater, or a reviler, or a drunkard, or a swindler—not even to eat with such a one. For what have I to do with judging outsiders? Do you not judge those who are within the church? But those who are outside, God judges. Remove the wicked man from among yourselves.
>
> 1 Corinthians 5:11–13

Appendix 3

Types and Symptoms of Child Sexual Abuse

Types of Abuse

The information given below is not all-inclusive. These lists of general types of abuse are divided into those that involve touching and those that do not.

Abuse That Involves Touching

fondling
physical stimulation or gratification
oral, genital, or anal penetration
intercourse with genitals or objects
rape
sadomasochism

Abuse That Does Not Involve Touching

lewd verbal comments
displaying or viewing of pornographic material, including but not limited to videos, magazines, and books
obscene or harassing phone calls
written or verbal communication of sexual or sexually suggestive nature (such as in on-line computer chat rooms, etc.)
allowing children to witness sexual activity by others, children or adult

Symptoms of Abuse

The information below is not all-inclusive. Although most abused or molested children evidence one or more of the following characteristics, it should not be assumed that any and all children who exhibit such characteristics have been abused.

Physical Signs May Include

lacerations and bruises
recurring nightmares
irritation, pain, regular discomfort, or injury to the genital area
difficulty sitting
torn or bloody underclothing
venereal or sexually transmitted disease

Behavioral Signs May Include

anxiety when approaching a child care area
nervous, hostile, or rejecting behavior toward one or more adults
sexual self-consciousness
acting out of sexual behaviors or other expressions of sexual knowledge beyond that appropriate for the child's age
withdrawal from church, school, or sports activities
withdrawal from friends and family

Appendix 4

Directory

Secular Organizations

The American Humane Association, Children's Division

63 Inverness Drive East
Englewood, CO 80112-5117
800-227-4645
The AHA serves as an information center on child protective services in the community. One of its goals is to build an aware and caring society for children and families. There is an abundance of informational publications available through the AHA.

American Professional Society on the Abuse of Children (APSAC)

407 Dearborn Avenue, Suite 1600
Chicago, IL 60605
312-554-0166
Fax: 312-554-0919

Center for Prevention of Sexual and Domestic Violence

206-634-1903
This organization produced the video documentary "Hear Their Cries: Religious Responses to Child Abuse." A study guide and brochures are included with purchase of video.

The Children's Advocacy Center

1110 East 32nd Street
Austin, TX 78722
512-472-1164
Fax: 512-472-1167

Church Mutual Insurance Company

3000 Schuster Lane
Merrill, Wisconsin 54452
This company has printed materials in booklet form on prevention of child sexual abuse. One of their wonderfully written booklets is titled "Safety Tips on a Sensitive Subject: Child Sexual Abuse." The CMIC serves as a resource for many churches.

Clearinghouse on Child Abuse and Neglect Information

P. O. Box 1182
Washington, D.C. 20013-1182
800-FYI-3366
The clearinghouse acts as a major resource for and disseminates infor-

mation to professionals and others concerned with child maltreatment and abuse.

Department of Child Protective Services

These groups are advocates for children. Their numbers can be found in local telephone directories. In some cases, the groups are located within the departments of Social Services. The CPS is a government organization which prints pamphlets warning against all forms of child abuse.

False Memory Syndrome Foundation

3401 Market Street, Suite 130
Philadelphia, PA 19104
800-568-8882
215-387-1865
Fax: 215-387-1917
There is controversy over the accuracy of distant memories of sexual abuse, especially those uncovered through counseling. This foundation assists those who claim to be wrongly accused of child abuse due to the false memories of others.

Interfaith Sexual Trauma Institute (ISTI)

Saint John's Abbey and University
Collegeville, MN 56321
612-363-3931
Fax: 612-363-2115
E-mail: Isti@csbsju.edu
The Interfaith Sexual Trauma Institute is a joint creation of Saint John's Abbey and University. Its leadership

board is an interdenominational group of men, women, victims, offenders, practitioners in the helping and legal professions, academicians, writers, and church leaders.

International Society for the Prevention of Child Abuse and Neglect (ISPCAN)

332 South Michigan Avenue,
Suite 1600
Chicago, IL 60604
312-663-3520
Fax: 312-939-8962

National Child Abuse Defense and Resource Center—Legal Help

419-865-0526
Fax: 419-865-0526
E-mail: ehm4m@virginia.edu
This agency can be helpful if one is involved in a child sexual abuse case with likely criminal implications.

National Committee to Prevent Child Abuse (NCPCA)

332 South Michigan Avenue,
Suite 1600
Chicago, IL 60604
800-342-7472
Fax: 312-939-8962

National Criminal Justice Reference Service

Box 6000
Rockville, MD 20850
800-851-3420
The NCJRS serves as an international clearinghouse for the exchange and

dissemination of information about criminal justice, including corrections, law enforcement, and juvenile justice. It also provides information on topics such as drugs, child abuse, and rehabilitation.

National Employment Screening Services, Inc.

8801 South Yale Street
Tulsa, OK 74137-3575
918-491-9936
NESS is the publisher of the book *The Guide to Background Investigations.*

Survivors and Victims Empowered (SAVE)

P. O. Box 10756
Lancaster, PA 17605-0756
717-569-3636
Fax: 717-581-1355
This organization has large resource data bases, which can be installed in many computer program managers.

Christian Organizations

American Association of Christian Counselors

2421 West Pratt Avenue, Suite 1398
Chicago, IL 60645
800-526-8673
E-mail:
102124.2061@compuserve.com

The Child Safety Program (CSP)

4800 Waco Drive
Waco, TX 75702-2518
MARET Systems International

Program codeveloped by MARET and Word, Inc., and marketed by Word, Inc.
800-933-9673, ext. 2037, reference number 03178
Cost for the program is approximately $130.
This program is individualized and uses a survey format. The ninety-six-page manual provides some detail on how to establish a safe church. Also included is a section on dealing with false accusations. The program allows applicants' screening information to be cataloged by computer, which enhances data searches.

Christian Ministry Resources

P. O. Box 1098
Matthews, NC 28106
704-841-8066
One of the best Christian legal organizations, CMR publishes the monthly Church Law & Tax Report for ministers and church leaders. It is on the cutting edge in the push for churches to implement formal screening procedures of its children's ministries workers.

Covenant House

NINELINE Counselors
800-999-9999
The Roman Catholic organization deals mostly with runaways who are living on the streets, many of whom have experienced sexual abuse. It can put a child in touch with people who can help them, in many cases right in their own hometown.

Local Covenant Houses:

Alaska
609 F Street
Anchorage, AK 99501

California
1325 North Western Avenue
Hollywood, CA 90027

Florida
733 Breakers Avenue
Fort Lauderdale, FL 33304

Louisiana
611 North Rampart Street
New Orleans, LA 70112

New Jersey
3529 Pacific Avenue
Atlantic City, NJ 08401

14 William Street
Newark, NJ 07102

New York
346 West 17th Street
New York, NY 10011

Texas
1111 Lovett Boulevard
Houston, TX 77006

Washington D.C.
P.O. Box 77764
Washington, DC 20013

Emerge Ministries, Inc.

900 Mull Avenue
Akron, OH 44313
330-867-5603
This organization produced video instruction on "Caring for the Family of God: Facing the Challenges of the '90s." Volume 2 of this series deals with child sexual abuse.

Focus on the Family

8605 Explorer Drive
Colorado Springs, CO 80920
800-932-9123
Focus on the Family is probably the strongest Christian advocate organization for the family in America today.

North American Association of Christians in Social Work

P. O. Box 7090
St. Davids, PA 19087-7090
215-687-5777

Wounded Heart Ministries

16075 West Belleview Avenue
Morrison, CO 80465
303-333-0066
This organization offers a helpful three-day seminar that addresses sexual abuse and recovery. It also can provide referrals to other local and national organizations.

National Hotlines

ChildHelp USA

I. O. F. Foresters National Child Abuse Hotline
P. O. Box 630
Hollywood, CA 90028
800-4-A CHILD
This group is located in Hollywood, California. It helps many hundreds of runaways annually. Some of its services include crisis phone counseling,

with local and national counseling referral services.

Division of Youth and Family Services

Office of Child Abuse Control (OCAC)
800-792-8610
This national hotline for reporting of sexual abuse or child neglect is accessible from the contiguous United States. Any call received at OCAC during normal working hours is referred immediately to the appropriate district office. Calls received after working hours are referred to and handled by the OCAC Special Response Unit.

The National AIDS Hotline

800-342-AIDS
800-244-SIDA (Español)
800-AIDS-TTY (TTY/TTD service for hearing-impaired)

National Center for Missing and Exploited Children

2101 Wilson Blvd., Suite 550
Arlington, VA 22201
800-843-5678
703-235-3900
800-826-7653 (hearing impaired line)

National Childwatch

4065 Page Avenue
P. O. Box 1368
Jackson, MI 49204
800-222-1464
This organization provides a national database of missing children. Any individual, private group, or state agency may report a missing child to be added to the database.

National Committee for Prevention of Child Abuse

800-55NCPCA
312-663-3520

The National STD Hotline

800-227-8922

Rape, Abuse, and Incest National Network (RAINN)

800-656-HOPE
RAINN is provided as a service to those who cannot reach or do not know of a local rape crisis center. It was founded by large grants from major recording companies in America.

Reporting Agencies and Survivor Organizations

The responsibility for investigating reports of suspected child abuse rests at the state level. As a result, each state has established a Child Protective Services (CPS) reporting system. This list is more specific than the national list provided earlier.

Alabama
Department of Human Resources
Division of Family and Children's Services
Office of Protective Services
Ripley Street
Montgomery, AL 36130-1801

National Resource Center on Child Sexual Abuse
107 Lincoln Street
Huntsville, AL 35801
800-543-7006

Alaska
Department of Health and Human Services
Division of Family and Youth Services
Box H-05
Juneau, AK 99811
800-478-4444 (in state only)
907-478-4444

American Samoa
Director, Department of Human Resources
American Samoa Government
Pago Pago, AS 96799

Arizona
Arizona Chapter/National Committee to Prevent Child Abuse
P. O. Box 63921
Phoenix, AZ 85082-3921
602-835-1411

Arizona Department of Economic Security
Administration for Children, Youth and Families, 940A
P. O. Box 6123
Phoenix, AZ 85005
602-542-3981

Arkansas
Arkansas Department of Human Services
Division of Children and Family Services
P. O. Box 1437

Little Rock, AR 72203
800-482-5964 (in state only)

California
Child Molester Identification Line
900-463-0400
Cost: $10 per call to check out two people.

Adults Molested as Children (AMAC)
P. O. Box 608
Pacific Grove, CA 93950
408-646-1855

CHILDHELP USA Child Abuse Survivor: A Prevention Program
1345 El Centro Avenue
P. O. Box 630
Hollywood, CA 90028

Department of Social Services
Office of Child Abuse Prevention
744 P Street, MS 19-82
Sacramento, CA 95814

Incest Survivors Anonymous (ISA)
P. O. Box 5613
Long Beach, CA 90807

Mothers Against Sexual Abuse (MASA)
503 South Myrtle Avenue, #4
Monrovia, CA 91016
818-969-0404

Norma J. Morris Center for Healing from Child Abuse
2306 Taraval Street, Suite 102
San Francisco, CA 94116-2252
415-564-6002

Olive Crest Treatment Center for Abused Children
1300 North Kellogg, Suite D
Anaheim, CA 92807

714-777-4999
Fax: 714-777-0278

Sexual Abuse Anonymous (SAA)
P. O. Box 9665
Berkeley, CA 94709

Survivors of Child Abuse Program
(SCAP)
1345 El Centro Avenue
P. O. Box 630
Hollywood, CA 90028
800-422-4453

Tamar's Voice
3130 Crow Canyon Road, Suite 260
San Ramon, CA 94583
510-275-0886

Colorado
Department of Social Services and
Child Welfare Services
25 East 16th Street
Denver, CO 80203-1702
(Make reports to County Departments
of Social Services.)

National Resource Center on Child
Sexual Abuse
63 Inverness Drive East
Englewood, CO 80112-5117
800-227-5242

Prevention and Treatment of Child
Abuse and Neglect
1205 Oneida Street
Denver, CO 80220
303-321-3963

Connecticut
Department of Children and Youth
Services
Division of Children and Protective
Services

70 Sigourney Street
Hartford, CT 06105
800-842-2248 (in state only)

Delaware
Department of Services for Children, Youth, and Their Families
Commission on Social Services
825 Faulkland Road
Wilmington, DE 19802
800-292-9582 (in state only)

District of Columbia
American Coalition for Abuse
Awareness
1858 Park Road NW, Second Floor
Washington, D.C. 20010
202-462-4688
Fax: 202-462-4689

Commission on Social Services
H Street Northeast
Washington, D.C. 20001
202-727-0995

National Center for Redress of
Incest and Sexual Abuse
1858 Park Road, First Floor
Washington, D.C. 20010
202-667-1160

National Center on Child Abuse
and Neglect: Clearinghouse Children's Bureau
Department of Health and Human
Services
P. O. Box 1182
Washington, D.C. 20013
800-394-3366

National Council on Child Abuse
and Family Violence
Washington Square

1155 Connecticut Avenue NW,
Suite 300
Washington, D.C. 20036
202-429-6695

Survivors of Catholic Clerical
Abuse (SOCCA)
Family Services Administration
P. O. Box 944
Washington, D.C. 20016-9411
202-537-0817

Florida
Department of Health and Rehabilitative Services
1317 Winewood Blvd.
Tallahassee, FL 32399-0700
904-487-4332

Florida Protective Service System
Fort Knox Blvd.
Tallahassee, FL 32308
800-342-9152 (in state only)

Georgia
Counseling Connection
P. O. Box 1935
Woodstock, GA 30188

Department of Human Resources
Peachtree Street, NW, Room 502
Atlanta, GA 30309

Guam
Child Welfare Services
Child Protective Services
P. O. Box 2816
Agana, GU 96910

Hawaii
Department of Human Services
Family and Adult Services
P. O. Box 339
Honolulu, HI 96809

Idaho
Field Operations Bureau of Social
Services and Child Protection
450 West State Street
Boise, ID 83720

Illinois
Child Abuse Prevention Programs
P. O. Box 265
Dolton, IL 60419

Child Sexual Abuse Treatment Center
345 Manor Court
Bolingbrook, IL 60439
708-739-0491

Department of Children and Fam-
ily Services
State Administration Offices
East Monroe Street
Springfield, IL 62701
800-25-ABUSE (in state only)

Illinois Coalition Against Sexual
Assault (ICASA)
Administrative Office
123 South 7th Street
Springfield, IL 62701
217-753-4117

LaCasa
1 South Greenleaf Street, Suite E
Gurnee, IL 60031
708-244-1187

North West Action Against Rape
870 East Higgins, Suite 136
Schaumburg, IL 60173
708-517-4488

Sister Survivor Support Services
Sr. Maureen Clancy SSND
537 Wesley Avenue
Evanston, IL 60202

Survivors Network of Those Abused by Priests (SNAP)
8025 South Honore
Chicago, IL 60620
312-483-1059

VOICES in Action (Victims of Incest Can Emerge Survivors)
P. O. Box 148309
Chicago, IL 60614
800-7-VOICE-8

Indiana

Department of Public Welfare— Child Abuse and Neglect
West Washington Street, Room W-364
Indianapolis, IN 46204

Iowa

Bureau of Adult, Children, and Family Services
Central Child Abuse Registry
Hoover State Office Building, Fifth Floor
Des Moines, IA 50319
800-362-2178 (in state only)

Kansas

Department of Social and Rehabilitation Services
Smith-Wilson Building
S. W. Oakley Street
Topeka, KS 66606
800-922-5330 (in state only)

Kentucky

Cabinet of Human Resources
Division of Family Services
East Main Street
Frankfort, KY 40621

Louisiana

Department of Social Services

Office of Community Services
P. O. Box 3318
Baton Rouge, LA 70821

Louisiana Council on Child Abuse
Parent Helpline: 800-348-KIDS
Parenting Center Warmline: 504-924-0123

Northeast Louisiana State University Resource Center
318-342-5437

Parenting Center at Children's Hospital Warmline
504-895-KIDS

Maine

Department of Human Services
Child Protective Services
State House, Station 11
Augusta, ME 04333
800-452-1999 (in state only)

Maryland

Baltimore Child Abuse Center
Child Advocacy Network
10 South Street, Suite 502
Baltimore, MD 21202
410-396-5165

Department of Human Resources
Social Services Administration
Saratoga State Center
West Saratoga Street
Baltimore, MD 21201

National Clearinghouse on Runaway and Homeless Youth
P. O. Box 13505
Silver Spring, MD 20911-3505
301-608-8098
Fax: 301-587-4352

National Victims Resource Center
Box 6000
Rockville, MD 20850-6000
800-627-6872

Survivors of Incest Anonymous (SIA)
P. O. Box 26870
Baltimore, MD 21212
410-433-2365

Massachusetts
Department of Social Services
Protective Services
Farnsworth Street
Boston, MA 02210
800-792-5200 (in state only)

Michigan
Association of Sexual Abuse Prevention Professionals (ASAP)
Box 421
Kalamazoo, MI 49005
616-349-9072

Department of Social Services
P. O. Box 30037
South Grand Avenue, Ste. 412
Lansing, MI 48909

National Childwatch
4065 Page Avenue
P. O. Box 1368
Jackson, MI 49204
800-222-1464

Sexual Abuse Survivors Anonymous
P. O. Box 241046
Detroit, MI 48224
313-882-6446

Sexual Assault Information Network of Michigan
517-832-0662

Minnesota
Department of Human Services
Children's Services Division
Human Services Building
St. Paul, MN 55155

Project Pathfinder, INC.
Griggs-Midway Building, Suite N385
1821 University Avenue West
St. Paul, MN 55104
612-644-8515

Sexual Abuse Survivors Services, Inc.
P. O. Box 591
Albert Lea, MN 56007
507-373-3655

Mississippi
Department of Human Resources
Office of Social Service Protection Department
P. O. Box 352
Jackson, MS 39205
800-222-8000 (in state only)

Missouri
Department of Social Service
Division of Social Services
P. O. Box 88
Broadway Building
Jefferson City, MO 65103
800-392-3738

Family Support Network
29 North Gore
St. Louis, MO 63119-2328
314-963-1450

Missouri Chapter—National Committee for the Prevention of Child Abuse
Jefferson City, MO 65103
573-634-5223

Missouri Division of Family Services
Jefferson City, MO 65103
573-751-2882

Survivors Support and Research
Network
P. O. Box 198
Fenton, MO
314-963-5241

Montana
Department of Family Services
Child Protective Services
P. O. Box 8005
Helena, MT 59604

Nebraska
Nebraska Department of Social
Services
301 Centennial Mall South
Lincoln, NE 68509
800-652-1999 (in state only)

Nevada
Department of Human Resources
Welfare Division
North Carson Street
Carson City, NV 89710
800-992-5757 (all counties except
Clark County)
702-399-0081 (Clark County)

New Hampshire
Division for Children and Youth
Services
Hazen Drive
Concord, NH 03301-6522
800-852-3345, ext. 4455 (in state only)

New Jersey
Child Abuse Hotline
The New Jersey Division of Youth
and Family Services (DYFS)

800-792-8610 (24 hours a day, 7 days
a week)
800-835-5510 (TTY/TDD for the hearing impaired)

Division of Youth and Family Services
Department of Human Services
(CN717)
East State Street, Sixth Floor
Trenton, NJ 08625
800-792-8610

International Network Against
Incest and Child Sexual Abuse
18 South Cadillac Drive
Somerville, NJ 08876
908-722-2933
Fax: 908-722-9665

Survivors of Abuse Find Empower-
ment (SAFE)
114 Bergerville Road
Freehold, NJ 07728
908-462-4412

New Mexico
Incest Survivors Resource Network
International (ISRNI)
P. O. Box 7375
Las Cruces, NM 88006-7375
505-521-4260
Fax: 505-521-3723

Protective Services Division
P. O. Drawer 5160
Pera Room 254
Santa Fe, NM 87502-5160
505-827-8400 (in state only)
Fax: 505-827-8480

Quaker Sexual Child Abuse Pre-
vention Network
Quaker SCAPnet
P. O. Box 7375

Las Cruces, NM 88006
505-521-4260
Fax: 505-521-3723

New York
Prevention Information Resource
Center Federation on Child Abuse
and Neglect
134 South Swan Street
Albany, NY 12210
518-445-1273

State Department of Social Services
Division of Family and Children
North Pearl Street
Albany, NY 12243
800-342-3720 (in state only)

North Carolina
Child Protective Services: A Branch
of Social Services
325 North Salisbury Street
Raleigh, NC 27603
919-733-2580
800-662-7030 (in state only)

Department of Human Resources
Careline: 800-662-7030 (in state only)

North Dakota
Department of Human Services
Division of Children and Family
Services
Child Abuse Neglect Program
East Boulevard
Bismarck, ND 58505

Ohio
Clearinghouse for Child Abuse
Prevention
2314 Auburn Avenue
Cincinnati, OH 45219
513-721-8932

Department of Human Services
Children's Protective Services
East Broad Street
Columbus, OH 43266-0423

National Organization on Male
Sexual Victimization (NOMSV)
918 South Front Street
Columbus, OH 43206
614-445-8277

Oklahoma
Child Protective Services
Division of Children and Family
Services
Department of Human Services
P. O. Box 25352
Oklahoma City, OK 73125
800-522-3511 (in state only)
405-521-2283

Oregon
Department of Human Resources
Children's Services Division
Commercial Street, Southeast
Salem, OR 97310
503-378-4722

Pennsylvania
Department of Public Welfare,
Children, Youth, and Families
Child Line and Abuse Registry
P. O. Box 2675
Harrisburg, PA 17105
800-932-0313 (in state only)

Good Tidings
Box 283
Canadensis, PA 18325
717-595-2705

Puerto Rico
Department of Social Services to
Families with Children

P. O. Box 11398
Puerto Rico 00910
809-724-1333

Rhode Island
Associates in Education and Prevention in Pastoral Practice
P. O. Box 63, 44 Main Street
North Kingstown, RI 02852
401-295-0698

Child Protective Services
Mt. Pleasant Avenue, Bldg. #9
Providence, RI 02908
800-RI-CHILD (in state only)

South Carolina
Department of Social Services
Confederate Avenue
P. O. Box 1520
Columbia, SC 29202-1520

South Dakota
Department of Social Services,
Child Protection Services
Governors Drive
Pierre, SD 57501

Tennessee
Department of Human Services
Child Protective Services
Citizen Bank Plaza
Deadrick St.
Nashville, TN 37248

Rape & Sexual Abuse Center of
Middle Tennessee, Inc.
56 Lindsley Avenue
Nashville, TN 37210
615-259-9055

Texas
Coalition for Advocacy and Accuracy About Abuse

Family Violence and Sexual
Assault Institute
1310 Clinic Drive
Tyler, TX 75701

Department of Human Services
Protective Services for Families
and Children Branch
P. O. Box 149030, C-E-206
Austin, TX 78714-9030
800-252-5400 (in state only)

Family Violence and Sexual
Assault Institute
1310 Clinic Drive
Tyler, TX 75701
903-595-6600

Utah
Department of Social Services
Division of Family Services
North 200 West
Salt Lake City, UT 84145-0500

Vermont
Department of Social and Rehabilitative Services
Division of Social Services
South Main Street
Waterbury, VT 05676
802-241-2131

Virgin Islands
Division of Children, Youth and
Families
Department of Human Services
Charlotte Amalie
St. Thomas, VI 00802
809-773-2323

Virginia
Abused Survivors Know, Inc. (ASK)
P. O. Box 10756

Burke, VA 22009
703-281-7468
Fax: 703-978-7395

Department of Social Services
Bureau of Child Protective Services
Clair Building
Discovery Drive
Richmond, VA 23229-8699
800-552-7096

National Center for Missing and
Exploited Children (NCMEC)
2101 Wilson Blvd., Suite 550
Arlington, VA 22201-3052
800-843-5678
Fax: 703-235-4067

National Center for Prosecution of
Child Abuse
American Prosecutors Research
Institute
99 Canal Center Plaza, Suite 510
Alexandria, VA 22314

Network for Professionals Concerned About Child Sexual Abuse
2501 North Glebe Road, Suite 202
Arlington, VA 22207

Washington
Department of Social and Health
Services,
Division of Children and Family
Services
Mail Stop OB 41-D
Olympia, WA 98504
800-562-5624 (in state only)

West Virginia
Department of Human Services
Office of Social Services
Building 6, Room 850

State Capitol Complex
Charleston, WV 25305
800-352-6513 (in state only)

Upper Ohio Valley Sexual Assault
Help Center
P. O. Box 6764
Wheeling, WV 26003
304-234-1783

Wisconsin
Department of Health and Social
Services
Bureau for Children, Youth, and
Families
West Wilson Street
P. O. Box 7851
Madison, WI 53707

Wyoming
Department of Family Services
Hathaway Building, #322
Cheyenne, WY 82002

Safehouse/Sexual Assault Services, Inc.
P. O. Box 1885
Cheyenne, WY 82003
307-637-7233

Canada
Institute for the Prevention of
Child Abuse
25 Spadina Road
Toronto, Ontario
Canada M5R 2S9
800-888KIDZ
Fax: 416-921-4997

Sexual Assault Recovery Anony-
mous (SARA)
P. O. Box 16
Surrey, British Columbia
Canada V3T 4W4

Internet Assistance and Research Groups

Self-help Christian and non-Christian groups researching ritual abuse:

http://www.xroads.com/rainbow/rahome.html
http://parc.power.net/users/aia
http://www.tardis.ed.ac.uk/~feorag/sram/sraindex.html
http://www.utu.fi/~jounsmed/asc/hyp/memories.html
http://user.aol.com/doughskept/witchhunt_links.html

Nongovernment informational resources on the prevention of child abuse:

http://www.med.umich.edu/aacap/
http://www.med.umich.edu/aacap/child.abuse.html
http://www.med.umich.edu/aacap/respond.child.abuse.html

To contact the project director of the child abuse prevention network at Cornell University: tph3@cornell.edu

Information or legal help from the National Child Abuse Defense Resource Center: ehm4m@virginia.edu

To request a booklet developed by the Mennonite Central Committee (MCC) that addresses the needs of persons indirectly affected by sexual abuse: mennonitecc.ca/mcc/pr/1995/10-06/8.

Information on a resolution passed by the General Board of Global Ministries, United Methodist Church (1996): gbgm-umc.org/mission/resolutions/sexabuse.

Notes

1. Stephanie Martin, "Who Will Protect the Children?" *Children's Ministry* (May/June 1995): 18–19.

2. America Online (AOL), Prodigy, and CompuServe are among those striving to curb unrestricted access to pornographic material on-line.

3. Statistics vary from agency to agency. This conclusion was drawn based on a child protective services fact sheet, "Know the Facts," (Arizona Department of Economic Security, 1994), 1–3. See also "Sexual Abuse: Who Should Report Child Abuse and Neglect?" America Online, Keyword: Online Psychology, 4 May 1996, 1.

Although definitions of child abuse vary from state to state, generally "child sexual abuse is criminal behavior that involves children in sexual behaviors for which they are not personally, socially, and developmentally ready," (Richard R. Hammar, Steven W. Klipowicz, and James F. Cobble Jr., *Reducing the Risk of Child Abuse in Your Church* [Matthews, N.C.: Christian Ministry Resources, 1993], 13).

4. Quoted by Craig Branch, "Public Education or Pagan Indoctrination," *Christian Research Journal,* (fall 1995): 34; taken from William J. Bennett, *The Index of Leading Indicators,* vol. 2 (Washington, D.C.: Empower America, The Heritage Foundation, 1993), 1.

5. Debbie Von Behren, *Baptist News Press,* 4 November 1995.

6. "Sex Abuse Tales Shock Hockey World," *The Bakersfield Californian,* 8 January 1997, D6.

7. In this book, the term *church* applies to any Christian ministry that utilizes children's workers. This includes churches, Christian schools, mission agencies, Bible school ministries, Christian clubs, etc. Each ministry will need to adapt the guidelines in this book to meet its unique ministry situation.

8. Hammar, Klipowicz, and Cobble, *Reducing the Risk,* 5.

9. The words *children* or *child* apply to anyone under the age of eighteen. *Children's ministries* are defined as those that encompass children from the crib room through seniors (under eighteen years of age) in the church's high school youth program.

10. Hammar, Klipowicz, and Cobble, *Reducing the Risk*, 11. This publication is part of an excellent video and book series released by Church Law and Tax Report Office.

Churches and organizations are coming out with official statements against abuse. The Council on Biblical Manhood and Womanhood (CBMW) released a statement that included, "We are against all forms of physical, sexual and/or verbal abuse." *CBMW News* 1, no. 1 (August 1995): 3.

11. An on-line computer news service reported that many Roman Catholics were leaving the church in Austria over the issue of one high-ranking leader's replacement. The replacement had been accused of sexual molestation and having homosexual tendencies.

12. "Ex-Pastor Refutes Sexual Assault Claims by 8 Women," *The Bakersfield Californian,* 9 December 1996, A5.

13. Bill Anderson, *When Child Abuse Comes to Church* (Minneapolis: Bethany House, 1992), 13.

14. Ibid.

15. Hammar, Klipowicz, and Cobble, *Reducing the Risk,* 15–16.

16. Jennifer King (pseudonym), regular correspondence with author, telephone, e-mail, and fax, 1995–96, Indianapolis, Indiana.

17. Ibid.

18. Mary Beth Jones (pseudonym), telephone interviews by author, summer 1996, Los Angeles, California.

19. Hammar, Klipowicz, and Cobble, *Reducing the Risk,* 15.

20. This is exactly what it took for one church. See Anderson, *When Child Abuse Comes to Church.*

21. Christian Legal Services, 708-383-2021. Church Law and Tax Report Office, Christian Ministry Resources, P.O. Box 1098, Matthews, N.C. 28106; telephone 704-841-8066, 800-222-1840.

22. A background check will tell if the person has registered as a sex offender in any state.

23. J. Oswald Sanders, *Spiritual Leadership* (Chicago: Moody Press, 1980); Francis M. Cosgrove, *Essentials of Discipleship* (Colorado Springs: NavPress, 1980).

24. It is wise to avoid the extremely flamboyant programs.

25. Seminary or training programs specifically in the area of safety issues are available from the Church Law and Tax Report Office, Christian Ministry Resources, P.O. Box 1098, Matthews, NC 28106; telephone 704-841-8066, 800-222-1840; or from the author, Ernest J. Zarra III, 400 Sinaloa Avenue, Bakersfield, CA 93312; telephone: 805-589-2025; e-mail: erzarra@zeus.kern.org.

26. For information, write to the Association of Christian Schools International, P. O. Box 4097, Whittier, CA 90607.

27. Roy B. Zuck, *Adult Education in the Church* (Chicago: Moody Press, 1970). Lawrence O. Richards, *A Theology of Christian Education*

(Grand Rapids: Zondervan, 1975). Howard Hendricks's series are available from Dallas Theological Seminary, 3909 Swiss Avenue, Dallas, TX 75204, 800-992-0998. *Leadership Journal,* P.O. Box 11618, Des Moines, IA 50340-1618; web site: http://www.christianity.net/leadership/6L3/html. *Christian Education Journal,* P.O. Box 650, Glen Ellyn, IL 60138.

28. Especially in larger churches, it is advisable to have sets of numbered badges to identify child with parent. Only by presenting a matching badge can an adult retrieve a child from the nursery. This helps avoid the problem of nursery workers who may not recognize each parent, and it gives parents the security of knowing that no one else can remove their child from the nursery.

29. Although insurance companies do not have set guidelines, many are adamant that the risk of liability increases any time children under the age of sixteen are allowed to act in a guardian role.

30. Older youth workers who did not graduate from high school would fit this category.

31. Arizona's definition of child sexual abuse is "the exploitation of a child or adolescent for the sexual gratification of another person. It includes behaviors such as intercourse, sodomy, oral-genital stimulation, verbal stimulation, exhibitionism, voyeurism, fondling, and involving a child in prostitution or the production of pornography." Child Protective Services, Arizona Department of Economic Security (1994), P.O. Box 44240, Phoenix, AZ 85064-4240, 800-330-1822.

32. Hammar, Klipowicz, Cobble, *Reducing the Risk,* 13.

33. National Resource Center on Child Sexual Abuse, correspondence with author via e-mail, November 1995.

34. This last point might be too much for the general public to handle at first. It might be wise to reserve this for a later media update after some of the emotional fervor has dissipated.

35. No sample statement is provided because the best words and style of presentation will be determined by the personality of each church or ministry. Ministry leadership should know their members well enough to decide the wisest way to handle this announcement.

36. The Directory of Organizations in appendix 4 provides some help in the search for counseling organizations. Referrals can also be obtained from the American Association of Christian Counselors, 800-5-COUN-SEL, http://199.227.69.135/aacc/html. There are also many hospitals and clinics in America that help victims to rebuild their lives. The Minirth-Meier New Life Clinics have programs nationwide: P.O. Box 850778, Richardson, TX 75085-0778, 800-NEWLIFE.

37. We should be clear that restoration ministry is the process by which

a body of believers comes alongside the repentant perpetrator, with the goal of assisting him or her toward health. This by no means implies restoration to a working ministry position.

38. Everett F. Harrison, ed., *Baker's Dictionary of Theology* (Grand Rapids: Baker Book House, 1960), 444.

39. See Beth Sterling, *The Thorn of Sexual Abuse* (Grand Rapids: Revell, 1994).

40. Anderson, *When Child Abuse Comes to Church*, 140–41.

41. Ibid., 143.

For Further Reading

Secular

Bass, Ellen, and Laura Davis. *The Courage to Heal.* New York: Harper & Row, 1988.

Davis, Laura. *The Courage to Heal Workbook.* New York: Harper & Row, 1990.

Crewdson, John. *By Silence Betrayed: Sexual Abuse of Children in America.* Boston: Little, Brown, & Co., 1988. Written in a popular journalistic style, this book helps the reader to understand the problem of sexual abuse in America.

Gardner, Richard. *Protocols for the Sex Abuse Evaluation.* Cresskill, N.J.: Creative Therapeutics, 1995.

———. *Psychotherapy with Sexual Abuse Victims: True, False and Hysterical.* Cresskill, N.J.: Creative Therapeutics, 1996. Both books by Gardner can be ordered by contacting the Creative Therapeutics group at 800-544-6162.

Gil, Eliana. *Outgrowing the Pain: A Book for and about Adults Abused as Children.* San Francisco: Launch, 1983.

Holman, Wendy, and Beverly Maltz. *Incest and Sexuality: A Guide to Understanding and Healing.* San Francisco: Jossey Bass, 1987.

Lew, Mike. *Victims No Longer.* New York: Harper & Row, 1990.

Loftus, Elizabeth, and Katherine Ketcham. *The Myth of Repressed Memory: False Memories and Allegations of Sexual Abuse.* New York: St. Martin's Press, 1994.

Long, Richard. *The Guide to Background Investigations.* Tulsa: National Employment Screening Services, Inc., 1989. The cost for this book is $95. It can be ordered by phoning 918-491-9936.

Nichols, Edward. *False Allegations of Child Sexual Abuse: The Attorney's Desk Reference.* Conway, S.C.: NCPI, Inc., n.d. This reference deals with the controversial topic of false accusations of child sexual abuse. Attorneys find it helpful as it points out the inner workings and weaknesses of child protective agencies as they deal with sexual abuse.

Sanford, Linda Tschirhart. *The Silent Children: A Parent's Guide to the Prevention of Child Sexual Abuse.* Garden City, N.Y.: Anchor Press/Doubleday, 1980. Although this book is somewhat dated, it contains tested strategies to protect children against sexual abuse.

Christian

Allender, Dan. *The Wounded Heart.* Colorado Springs: NavPress, 1990. This is an important book for adult survivors of abuse and those who care about them.

Anderson, Bill. *When Child Abuse Comes to Church.* Minneapolis: Bethany House, 1992. To inform Christians that child abuse does occur in churches, the author details an account of child sexual abuse at one of the churches he pastored.

Child Protection Program Foundation. *Victim Services Resource Manual: For Pastors and Lay Leaders.* 7441 Marvin D. Love Freeway, Suite 200, Dallas, Tex. 75237. This helpful manual contains lists of Christian and secular groups and organizations, along with brief descriptions of each.

Draper, Perry. *Haunted Memories.* Grand Rapids: Revell, 1996. The author, a licensed therapist, offers help for victims of abuse and those close to them. He handles tough topics, including satanic ritual abuse and dissociative identity disorder.

Heitritter, Lynn, and Jeanette Vought. *Helping Victims of Sexual Abuse*. Minneapolis: Bethany House Publishers, 1989. This excellent tool for Christian counselors contains precise strategies that can help victims and their families move down the road toward healing.

Klipowicz, Steven W. *Reducing the Risk of Child Sexual Abuse Training Manual*. Matthews, N.C.: Church Law & Tax Report, 1993. This manual provides an excellent way to lead a group in laying out procedures of children's ministries screening. Also included are steps to understanding the differences between paid workers and unpaid workers in a church setting.

Tesch, Wayne, and Diane Tesch. *Unlocking the Secret World: A Unique Christian Ministry to Abused, Abandoned, and Neglected Children*. Wheaton: Tyndale House, 1995. Can be ordered by telephoning 800-323-9400.

Quick List of 800 Numbers

American Association of Christian Counselors
800-526-8673

Center for Missing and Exploited Children
800-843-5678

Child Find Hotline
800-I-AM-LOST (800-426-5678)

ChildHelp USA
800-4-A-CHILD (800-422-4453)

Family Forum Library
800-99-YOUTH (800-999-6884)

Hit Home: Youth Crisis Hotline for Reporting Abuse and Help for Runaways
800-HIT-HOME (800-448-4663)

Hotline for Parents Considering Abducting Their Children
800-A-WAY-OUT (800-292-9688)

National Runaway Hotline
800-231-6946

National Youth Crisis Hotline
800-442-HOPE (800-442-4673)

Operation Lookout: National Center for Missing Youth
800-782-SEEK (800-782-7335)

Parents Reporting Lost Children Hotline
800-426-5678

Runaway Teens Hotline (Covenant House)
800-999-9999

Survivors United Network
800-456-HOPE (800-442-4673)